Echoes of Ambleside
and beyond

Reminiscences and recollections
of an Ambleside octogenarian

George Middleton

Edited by Brian Mace

I am most grateful for the help and encouragement given to me by Anne Glaister in bringing this book to life.

I am much indebted to Brian Mace for editing and designing this book.

George Middleton
October 2012

Photographs

Many of the photographs are from the author's own collection. These are denoted by the initials GM.

The copyright of the other photographs and on the cover, and of the maps, is held by Brian Mace.

First published in England in 2015 by Brian Mace, Church View, Vicarage Road, Ambleside, LA22 9DH.

Printed by MTP Media Ltd, The Sidings, Beezon Fields, Kendal, LA9 6BL
www.mtp-media.co.uk

Cover photographs: main background - Rothay Park, Ambleside, in the autumn; front cover - George in his pram (GM), George and his dog Ben in Rothay Park, and Bridge House, Ambleside; back cover - George (GM)

Contents

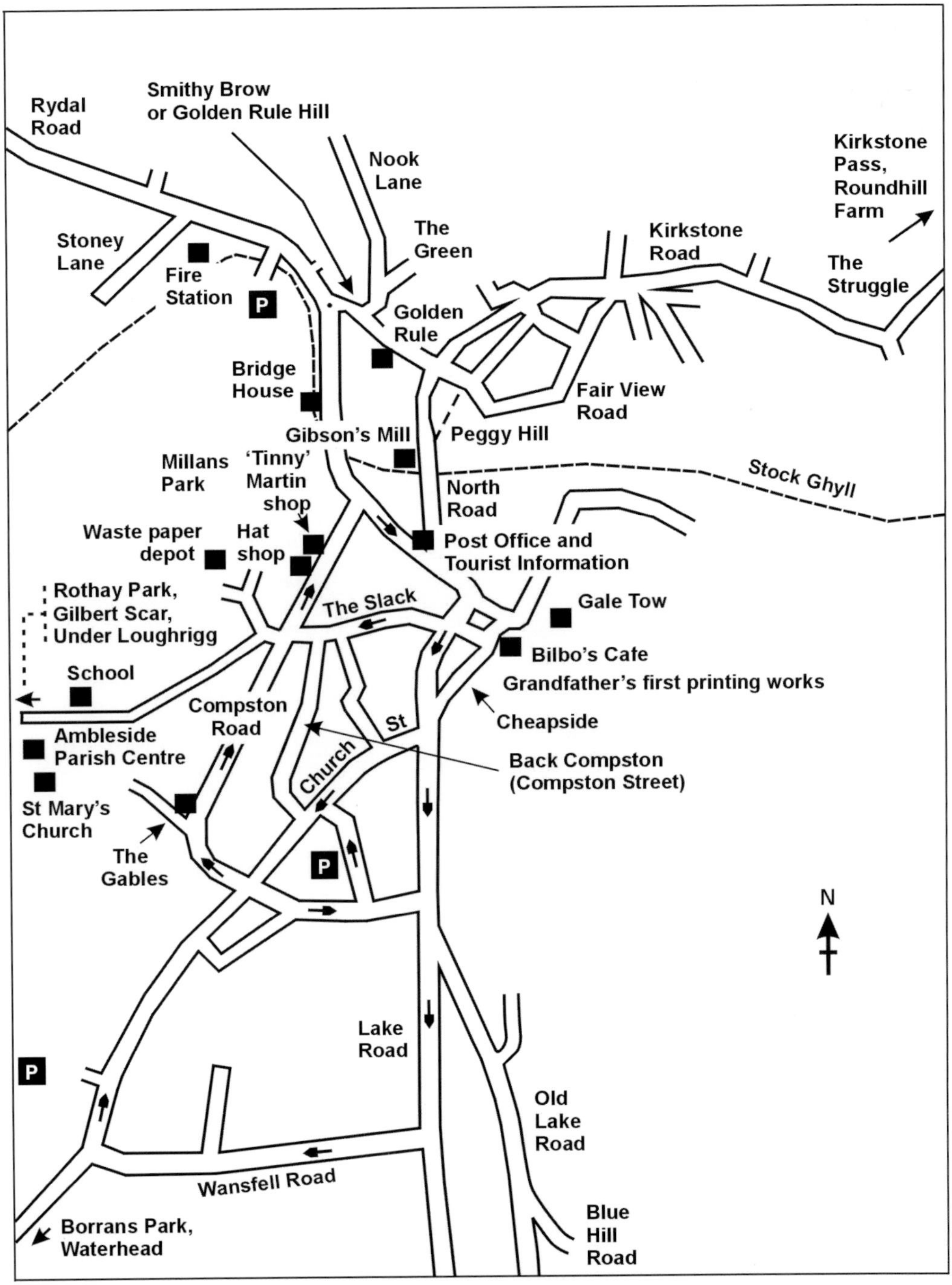

Ambleside
Places mentioned in the book,
and points of reference

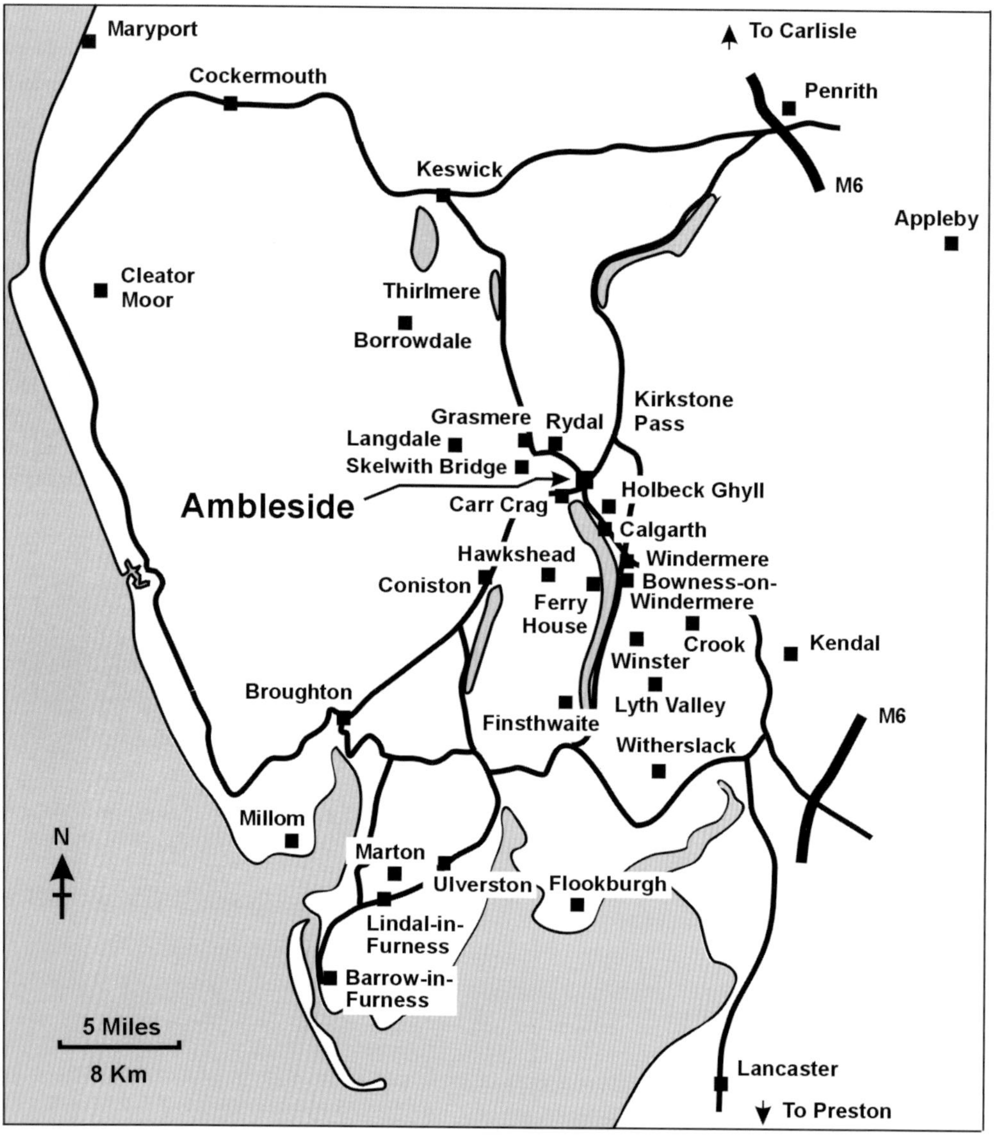

Places mentioned in the book,
and points of reference

Preface

I was a gardener all my working life, though I did spend several weeks working in a shop in Kendal during one particularly bad winter, and I continue to be closely interested in gardening even now.

The events described in this book are as I remember them or as I remember them being told to me. Many of these memories came from my father. I can see him now in my mind's eye, sitting by the open fire in the evening and sucking gently on his pipe as he talked to me of times past. For example, from the days of his boyhood he recalled the early story of Chippy Davis. I remember buying fish and chips from Chippy and his wife Bessie in the days of my own boyhood.

I am well aware that other people may have different memories of these same events.

The reminiscences and recollections are generally presented as separate short stories, each one in its own right. I hope they will rouse curiosity and maybe bring you to Ambleside to have a look round for yourself. Or are you already a visitor who will discover something new?

It is inevitable that some of the buildings featured in this book have been changed since the times to which the memories are relevant but the buildings retain their place in my own part of history.

I hope that all the names mentioned are spelled correctly. If any of them are not, I apologise.

George Middleton
October 2012

My grandparents Park, William and Mary. GM

My grandparents Middleton, George and May. GM

Chapter 1 **Great grandparents and grandparents**

When the parents of my Granddad Bill Park lived at Crook in a hovel made with stones, tin sheets and turf, and not in a house, they had farmers help them build a one-bedroom cottage. It was called Owert Beck. It had no water supply except from the stream close by.

In times of frost and snow, quite often it was like that for many weeks. There was no fridge in those days so they kept a sack of food in the stream, sometimes covered in moss, to keep the family in food for as long as possible.

There was no garden, so great grandma used the sides of the road. She grew gooseberries, raspberries, blackcurrants, redcurrants and many other fruits there. Two goats were tethered there as well. She collected grass seeds off the roadside like the gypsies used to do, and various leaves from trees which she dried. She collected wild oats, wild barley and wild corn from the roadside to be stored in tall clay urns with wooden lids. Damsons were collected from the roadside trees and she made jam with them. She kept hens, and used to sell eggs and fruit on the roadside. Although the lord of the manor objected to her doing this and attempted to stop her by various means, he did not succeed. She kept her stall by the roadside right through her life.

Owert Beck, no longer a one-bedroom cottage.
This building is over the beck (owert beck) when travelling from Crook to Kendal.

Great grandfather Park worked in the lead mine at Crook until it closed, and then moved to Ambleside to work in the lead mine at Kirkstone. Sometimes he used to walk to the lead mines daily until the owners built hog houses to stay in. The workers stayed there for the week.

But there was still no guarantee of work. The men would line up each morning for the boss to select which of them would work that day. "Thou's to work." he would say to each man as he was selected.

If there was generally no work at the lead mine, he would go to the copper-mines at Coniston. He also worked sometimes at the graphite mine in the Borrowdale Valley.

He used to have to make tallow candles as they worked by candlelight in the mines until they got paraffin and other kinds of lamps.

Grandpa Park used to tell me that they moved to Moor Cottage at Carkettle near Marton, which is near Lindal in Furness. The iron ore pits were there; they moved into the foreman's house and brought up their family there until all of them left school and went to be hired in various jobs. He was a shot fixer and gunpowder man.

He was hired for blasting out the rock to make way for the new pipeline which would take water from Thirlmere to Manchester, and he helped in blasting the new river channel when Stock Ghyll was diverted to its present course round Rothay Park in Ambleside.

Grandma Middleton, May Coffee, was born at The Haven on Rydal Road. There used to be photographs of her in the Queen's Hotel in Ambleside wheeling two boys in a pram and three boys walking: Uncle Fred and Uncle Frank were in the pram and Uncle Harry, Uncle Billy and my father were walking by the pram. The Fern family had the Queens Hotel at that time. The photographs were removed during the latest refurbishment of the hotel.

Red on tha boots

While walking over the Kirkstone Pass and Fell, Grandfather Bill used to set traps on his way to and from work to catch various creatures such as rabbits, hares and pheasants. On his way home he would colllect what had been caught.

During a particularly bad time, Grandfather Bill had no money and there was no food at home for the family. He thought long and hard as he climbed The Struggle one morning to the top of Kirkstone Pass.

He noticed the sheep in the fields – how many there were. And the thought came to him that he might kill one to provide some meat. Just one would not be missed. But killing one would not be the proper thing to do.

On the way home he did catch a sheep and kill it. Carrying the carcase would not have been easy for him so he cut off the four legs and then buried the rest of the carcase so that birds, foxes and other creatures would not find it for food for themselves. He tied the legs to the ends of two pieces of string, and put one string over each shoulder so that the legs hung down in front of and behind him, and put his coat on to hide them.

When he got down into the town, the local police sergeant was standing at one of the road junctions. He greeted grandfather pleasantly and asked him how he was getting on. Grandfather replied that things were not at all good.

During the short conversation, the sergeant had looked at grandfather's boots and then asked: "What's that red on tha boots? Open tha coat."

Grandfather had to reveal the four sheep's legs, and explained what he had done.

"I will have to arrest you and keep you in the police station over night." said the sergeant.

Next morning, grandfather appeared in court charged with killing a sheep. He was, of course, guilty but he asked the judge if he could speak with the judge in private and not in front of the other people in the courtroom. The judge agreed and the courtroom was cleared.

After the two men had talked together, the judge called the court to assemble once again. After everyone was back in their places, the judge said that he had decided that grandfather should go free. The case was closed.

--- ooooo ---

My Grandparents Middleton, George and May, with their five boys Thomas (my Father), Frank, Billy (standing), Fred and Harry. GM

The premises in Cheapside where Grandfather George opened his printing business.
Bilbo's cafe is upstairs and the outdoors pursuits shop downstairs.

Chapter 2 **Grandfather's printing business, and how the Little Echo newspaper got its name**

My grandfather George started his printing business in Cheapside, and called it the St Oswald Press. The name was chosen because of some connection he had with Grasmere which I do not remember. The church at Grasmere is dedicated to St Oswald.

Grandfather was able to have an electricity supply for the printing works by laying a cable from a turbine in Stock Ghyll. The turbine had been built by Mr Grimes to supply his workshop which was closeby and his house on Gale Tow, now Gale Terrace, which he also built.

One of grandfather's best customers was Charlotte Mason from the college she founded in Ambleside. Other good customers were the King's School in Ambleside and the Huyton Hill School on the road to Hawkshead. He also printed the score cards for the tournaments at the big houses around the district, and the score cards for the golf tournament and the clock golf. My father and his brothers used to go around the district collecting the scores. On one occasion while collecting the scores from the Heelis family, he met the housekeeper who was doing the same sort of thing as himself – etching information on to copper plates. He got very friendly with her and started to take her out. She used to go to the printing works to meet him.

That lady was the housekeeper of Mrs William Heelis, who is known famously around the world by another name – Beatrix Potter, the creator of the Peter Rabbit stories.

Later, my father started to help Herbert Bennett at Roundhill Farm by doing various odd jobs for him. They also enjoyed a pint together in a local pub. It was at Roundhill Farm that my father met Hilda Park for the first time. Romance blossomed and Herbert was not too pleased because he could see what was going to happen: he would be losing Hilda. The wedding took place at Lindal Church on 5 September 1925.

Some time after 1925, grandfather moved the printing works to larger premises at Stock Ghyll, to where the Silver Moon business is today in North Road.

In due course, the premises in Cheapside became Mammy Rae's sweet and toy shop, a general store in fact. Later, Mr and Mrs Bill Kent had a toy shop there. Later still it became Wilf's cafe, and now it is Bilbo's cafe and a shop which sells clothing and equipment for outdoor activities.

The Silver Moon premises in North Road.

Further expansion of grandfather's business resulted in the lack of space once more. Grandfather and the father of Charles Gibson were great friends. One day, Charles' father and grandfather were in conversation.

"Now, Sketcher (my grandfather's nickname), how are you doing?"

"OK, but I'm getting cramped for space again."

"What about my redundant mill? A bit of a ruin but it could be rebuilt."

"How much do you want for it?"

"How about £20? You will need permission from the lord of the manor."

Grandfather went to see Mr Le Fleming at Rydal Hall. He agreed to grandfather's use of the site provided the new building was of tin (corrugated iron) and painted green. Grandfather said that tin was not suitable for a printing works so the building would be lined with timber.

He produced stationery for many of the local hotels and businesses. These included the Heelis law firm in Hawkshead and Ambleside.

And grandfather did one special job for Beatrix Potter (Mrs Heelis): 100 copies of her book "The Fairy Caravan".

Among the many things which grandfather printed were the magazines for local churches. Some things were printed on behalf of other companies. And he produced tiny Bibles for other companies, so tiny that a very small magnifying glass was included inside the back cover so that the text could be read.

One of the tiny Bibles and its leather-mounted magnifying glass.
The pages measure 1.14 inches by 1.67 inches (29mm by 42.5mm); the last one is numbered 876. Including its leather cover, the Bible is 0.6 inches thick, 15mm.

When grandfather gave up running the business it was taken over by Uncle Fred and my father.

The Little Echo

One of my grandfather's favourite places for a walk, where he took the family, was to go up to Rydal and then continue up the valley past Rydal Hall and Nab Farm to Buxton Jump.

Grandma and granddad were walking in the Rydal Valley one afternoon with the boys when granddad stopped, turned to grandma and said: "I think I will print a little newspaper for Ambleside, May."

She said: "Don't you think you have enough work to do, with the Charlotte Mason college printing, Huyton Hill School, King's School and other work for businessmen in Ambleside and the surrounding area? If you printed a newspaper, what would you call it?"

"I haven't given it much thought," he said.

As they walked a bit further up the valley he stopped, turned to grandma and said: "Did you hear that, May? That's what I am going to call the newspaper."

Grandma asked: "What do you mean?"

"Listen as you walk along."

"Do you mean that echo going through the valley?" she asked.

"Yes, that's right. The Little Echo. That's what I am going to call it, if I print it."

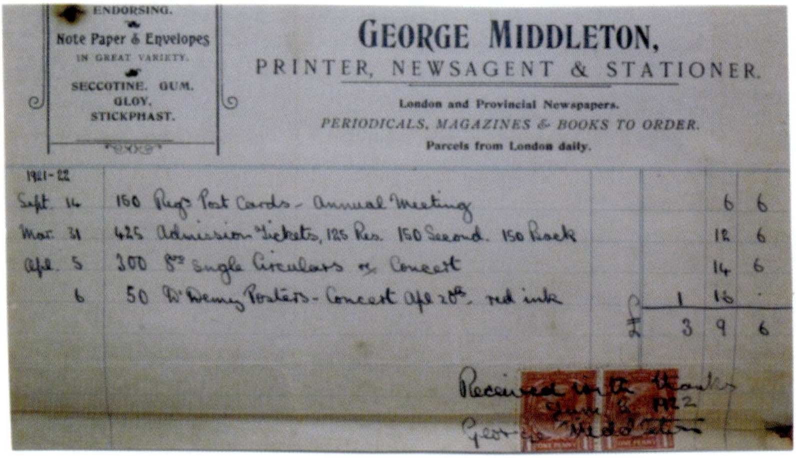

ENDORSING.
Note Paper & Envelopes
IN GREAT VARIETY.
SECCOTINE. GUM.
GLOY.
STICKPHAST.

GEORGE MIDDLETON,
PRINTER, NEWSAGENT & STATIONER.
London and Provincial Newspapers.
PERIODICALS, MAGAZINES & BOOKS TO ORDER.
Parcels from London daily.

		£	s.	d.
1921-22				
Sept. 14	150 Reg. Post Cards - Annual Meeting		6	6
Mar. 31	425 Admission Tickets, 125 Res. 150 Second. 150 Back		12	6
Apl. 5	300 8vo Single Circulars re Concert		14	6
6	50 Dr Demy Posters - Concert Apl 20th. red ink	1	16	-
		£ 3	9	6

Received with thanks
Jun 8 1922
[illegible]

A receipt from 1922 bearing my grandfather's signature.

--- ooooo ---

Chapter 3 **Charlotte Mason**

When Charlotte Mason got off the train at Windermere, she asked the porter where she could hire a pony and trap to drive to Ambleside. He replied: "If you go down into Windermere you will see several pony and traps standing ready to go to Ambleside. You can drive yourself or Mr Jack Elleray will drive for you." She drove herself.

She stopped a gentleman named Mr Hindmoor in the street and asked him where there were any large houses in Ambleside, large enough to use as a school. He answered that the person she needed to speak to was the local printer called Mr George Middleton (my grandfather). She went to the print works and found him.

"I have been informed by a gentleman in the street named Mr Hindmoor that you are the person that will know more about houses in Ambleside which are for sale."

"Yes, madam," was his reply, "If you can wait until I have finished what I am doing, I will take you and show you the houses that I know are on the market. There are some on The Gale, in Old Lake Road, some in Skelghyll Woods, one or two under Loughrigg, and out at Brathay, on Rydal Road and at Rydal. Other houses are Meadow Bank, Springfield, Scale How, Low Nook, and some up North Road and Kirkstone Road."

When he had finished the job in hand, he took her to see Meadow Bank, Springfield, Scale How and Low Nook. When they had finished, he took her to the house in North Road where they lived and met Grandma and her two sisters the Miss Coffees.

Charlotte Mason purchased Low Nook and established the House of Education at Scale How.

Three of the principals at what later became known as Charlotte Mason College were Miss Pickering, Miss Collins and Miss Trebenzie.

I started work at the college when I left school, under the supervision of the head gardener Mr Flitters, for £1 a week.

--- ooooo ---

Chapter 4 **White with mushrooms**

When Ambleside was white with mushrooms, white as snow, people gathered them gladly. Grandfather George loved them and there was always enough to fill a frying pan. How did they come about? Why was it that there were so many of them? The large numbers of horses and ponies used every day left a lot of manure along the roads. The manure found its way naturally to the sides of the roads, along the verges into the crevices in the walls, and in some places on to the rooftops. These places became very fertile for the mushroom spores to grow. They did so in profusion when the conditions were right.

It is a different world now. Weedkillers and treatments are used in the hay fields; rich mixtures of plants no longer grow.

People put chemicals on the land then.

--- ooooo ---

Features of Ambleside

The horse trough in Rothay Road.

The inscription across the top of the horse trough reads

Ho, everyone that thirsteth

It was very appropriate because two metal mugs used to hang above the trough on the righthand side, for use by anyone who needed a drink. The mugs and their hooks were eventually removed to reduce noise. Not because the mugs being used but because they made a lot of noise when banged against the stonework by young people.

The inscription on the panel behind the trough C S R March 25th 1878 refers, I think, to a member of the Routledge family who were well-known dealers in horses and ponies.

The inscription on the panel on the front of the trough LUDC 1946 refers to the Lakes Urban District Council. It came into being when I was very small, and ceased to exist when South Lakeland District Council came into being during the 1970s.

--- ooooo ---

Chapter 5 **Coffees the greengrocers: Aunt Agnes and Aunt Anne**

My aunts had a greengrocer and herbalist shop in North Road. From the fields, roadsides and hedgerows, burnups and other things were collected. Dog journals grew there; they looked like little knobbly potatoes. Herbs were collected as were 'weeds' such as nettles and various varieties of dockings. Fruit was collected from trees: elderberries, thornberries, mountain ash berries, sloes, apples, pears, plums and damsons. Various leaves and saps were also collected for use in the mixtures and remedies they made. The shop was well supplied with ingredients. People travelled far and wide to collect things for my aunts.

“There is no such thing as a weed,” they used to say, “because nearly everything that grows has a use.”

My father spent quite a lot of his spare time in the shop. He helped put things into their packages. Tea arrived in large wooden tea chests and had to be weighed out into packets. Peas and beans came in boxes and were also weighed out. Flour came in sacks from Gibson's Mill down the road.

My aunts were very much involved with the Primrose League which they founded together with Mrs Ethel Hedley from Brierly Close, Miss Hough from White Craggs, and the MacIver family from Waterhead Range.

The Haven on The Green, home of great grandfather Jeremiah Coffee and his wife.

Many years later, the farmer Mr Woodend and his wife retired here. He kept pigs in the outhouse.

Chapter 6 **Woodrow Wilson, the man from America**

An American man came down into Ambleside from the Kirkstone Pass on his bicycle and stopped outside my grandfather's printing office. He went into the works, and this started a friendship with my grandfather, and my father and his brothers, especially Billy the eldest brother. Woodrow also visited The Haven on The Green in Ambleside where lived Jeremiah Coffee and his wife, my grandma's father and mother.

Woodrow often popped in to my Aunt Coffees' grocers shop in North Road for medicinal remedies which were, of course, herb based. One day he fell off his bicycle and cut his leg. He made straight for the shop and they dressed the wound for him. And so began a close friendship with the Miss Coffees.

He came to Ambleside several times and also went to Carlisle where his grand-parents lived.

My Aunt Coffees built the bungalow by Stock Bridge in North Road. The Wills family took over their shop when they retired and they had Woodrow stay with them in the bungalow sometimes. When it was necessary to empty the bungalow some years later, a bicycle Woodrow had used together with those of my aunts and Uncle Billy had to be thrown away. They had been in the cellar for a long time and were completely rusty. Water from Stock Ghyll had been getting into the cellar and then seeping out again. On rare occasions, the water level was high enough to flood the bungalow as well as fill the cellar.

Woodrow never failed to go up on to Loughrigg by Browhead Farm and to Loughrigg Brow to see the wildlife up there including newts, lizards, deer, grouse, and pheasants.

--- ooooo ---

Ash Tree Cottage, round the corner from the top of Peggy Hill.
The entrance porch still has a bench on each side.

The top of Peggy Hill.
Chippy and Bessie lived in the nearest house on the right.

Chapter 7 **'Chippy' Davis**

Itinerant traders, known locally as roadsters, used to visit Ambleside. Some of them came regularly. The usual pattern was for them to spread a tarpaulin or something similar on the ground in front of the Salutation Hotel which used to be the market area and display their wares on it. For example, my grandfather had a hard-wearing, thorn-proof suit made by one of them. A Mr Martin was one of them. He eventually opened a tailor's shop on Lake Road next door to the district bank. The area was also used for circuses and other entertainments,

Another of the roadsters became known locally as 'Chippy' Davis. His real name was Walter, and he was of Welsh descent. He was always smartly dressed with collar and tie even though he slept rough out of doors on a bench, on the bank of Stock Ghyll near where the fire station is. (The next bench was occupied sometimes by a large Russian man who slept between two large black, performing bears.) Chippy's wares were not laid out on the ground but arranged on a large wheel. Most of them cost 1d (less than ½p). So it was that he did not follow the usual pattern of staying in front of the Salutation Hotel but went round the streets instead with his wares.

As time passed, Chippy became better known. A Mrs Woodburn lived at Ash Tree Cottage at the top of Peggy Hill. From time to time she gave him a cup of tea and sometimes cake as well. He enjoyed these while sitting in the porch at the front door. Occasionally, when the weather was bad, Mrs Woodburn invited him into the kitchen. With winter approaching, she persuaded him to stay at Ash Tree Cottage during his time in Ambleside – he slept in the kitchen on a makeshift bed. The house was quite full: Mrs Woodburn had seven children, six of them boys.

It might have been thought that he would start a relationship with Mrs Woodburn but it was the daughter Bessie who caught his eye. In due course, Walter and Bessie got married and lived at the top of Peggy Hill. Walter ceased his itinerant business and worked for several people. He was able to 'turn his hand' to many things.

Fish and chips? That is where the nickname came from. They converted part of their home into a fish and chip shop. Customers were sometimes so many that Chippy would ask Bessie to shut the door to keep them out while those inside waited for their orders to be cooked. I well remember being a customer myself as a youngster.

Bessie encouraged him to seek election to the Lakes Urban District Council. He did become a councillor, and he was its chairman for several years. He was popular enough to be usually elected unopposed.

--- ooooo ---

The newsagent and bed and breakfast business at the bottom of Church Street.

The Old Post Office at Winster. No space for a pavement.

Chapter 8 **My uncles, and some aunts**

My Uncle Billy was the first person to drive a bus into Ambleside. It was named 'The Yellow Peril' and was garaged in Wansfell Road near where the Roman Catholic Church is today.

The Osliffe family lived in Ambleside. Tommy's sister Louie married Uncle Billy. They lived at the shop at the bottom of Church Street, and ran a bed and breakfast business there as well (just as today). They had three boys and a girl. The girl was born in June and called June. Eventually, Uncle Billy and Aunty Louie moved up to Blue Hill.

June was a hairdresser in Ambleside and married a Canadian named John Nabb. They had three children in Canada.

The eldest Osliffe son was called Goodwin; he had a twenty-five piece band on the Isle of Wight each summer. The other two sons had a business in the Lakes area.

Tommy's daughter married Uncle Fred's son Stephen.

My Uncle Harry Middleton actually married a Middleton; she worked at Rydal Hall.

Uncle Percy worked at Loughrigg Brow house in the gardens for almost all of his working life, and continued into his eighties.

Uncle Frank married May Elleray and lived at Winster Post Office. That was until Lord Wakefield's father left him some land and property with two houses. He gave one to his son and the other to his daughter.

Aunty May's sister also lived at the post office and helped to run it very ably although she was blind. She knew where everything was.

After the great train robbery in 1963, the authorities thought that keeping the post office open was too big a risk, and closed it.

--- ooooo ---

My father Thomas, also known as Nevvy and as Elleray. GM

My parents' wedding. GM

Chapter 9 **My Father**

My father and his brothers were all born at the printing works which was sited in Cheapside behind the Market Clock.

Bronco Hardy went into the print works a day or two before Dad was getting married on the following Saturday. "Now then, Nevvy, how are you getting on?"

"I'm getting on fairly well, but I'm getting married on Saturday and I don't know where we are going to live." said my father.

Bronco said: "You've no need to worry, Nevvy. I have a yan (one) bed-roomed house under Gilbert Scar. You can have it for three and a tanner a week (three shillings and sixpence, or 17½ pence in modern currency). After you have finished work, come along and have a look at it. You don't need to worry about furniture or bedding for the beds and everything are there. The pots and pans are there too."

My parents first home was Gilbert Scar Cottage. Much extended since, the cottage was just the part where the creeper is growing up the wall.

When my mother became pregnant they had to find a new home. Captain Pickup had inherited a number of houses in the Millans Park area. Some of them were empty. Uncle Harry and Aunty Doris were already living at number 5 Park Street. Captain Pickup and my father went round to look at the empty houses.

They decided on number 6, at 5 shillings a week rent (25p). A few weeks after my father and mother moved in, Wood View became empty. Mother liked that better than number 6 because it had more rooms. So they asked if they could move to Wood View. Captain Pickup agreed, with the same rent of 5 shillings a week and the rates (local taxes) at 10 shillings.

The Saturday Penny

(In this episode, 12 pennies were the equivalent of the modern 5p.)

On a Saturday when we were young, we used to line up on Stock Bridge around lunchtime – about 12 o'clock – and wait for my father to come out from the printing works. He used to give each of us a Saturday penny: my eldest sister Mary and sisters Ann, Vera and Phyllis, me, and my brother Frank. Then we would change the penny that each of us received into half farthings (8 for each penny) and go into Mrs Holme's sweet shop which was part of the old mill waterwheel property. There we would buy some sweets for a farthing. When we came out she would say to us that there were fruit on the lefthand side: apples, pears, plums, peaches, grapes, and other kinds depending on the season, which were slightly damaged. "You can help yourselves to them. I would rather let you children have them instead of throwing them away. Your mother has been a good customer of mine, also your grandmother and grandfather, your Uncle Fred and Aunty Mabel. But don't touch the fruit on the righthand side."

A half farthing.

We also shopped at the grocery and sweet shop of Mrs Woodburn. This was in North Road, opposite where Fred Garside's butcher's shop is now. The

Woodburns also travelled around Ambleside with a vegetable and fruit van; Mrs Hodgson used to help them.

The bull in a pub

Few people knew that my father used to help butcher animals for local farmers.

One Saturday when he was supposed to go to Nook End Farm to kill the mad bull for Mr Woodend, his father said to him on arrival at the printing works,
"I'm sorry, Elleray, but you will have to work this morning as we have quite a backlog of work from the college to do." So he sent word to the farm that he would have to come later in the day or on Sunday morning.

Mr Woodend sent word in reply that the bull was too mad to keep alive until later so he had contacted Hebert Grizedale and he had said he would kill the bull.

Herbert went to kill the bull but did not stun it enough. It got up, smashed through the door of the shed, turned down Nook Lane, broke through three gates, and ended up on Golden Rule Hill (Smithy Brow). It turned to go down to the main road but was confronted by Brown's coach coming up the hill. So it turned to go up the road and was faced with Tom Bell coming down in his butcher's van. It turned again, and went into the Golden Rule pub. Breaking down the stained glass door, it landed on the floor in front of the bar. Everybody there rushed out through the back door. Scattering things everywhere, the bull got up again, broke through another door and skidded to the floor in the toilets.

Albert Faulkner, Brate Black and Tom Cat Woodburn arrived at the print works. "Elleray, you had better come with your gear as the bull has escaped from the farm and is in the bar of the Golden Rule."

My father thought they were 'having him on' which was not unusual but Albert said it was no joke. "The bull has broken through the door and is snorting in the bar."

My father asked my grandfather if he could go.

"Yes, you had better go."

My father collected his gear and went up to the Golden Rule. When he got there the bull was lying in the toilets and that is where he killed it.

The Golden Rule public house.

The customers were most grateful when they at last returned to the bar to finish their drinks.

With all the people buying my father drinks, he ended up "legless", unable to walk. Walter Crossland went and fetched a wheelbarrow, put him into it, and took him home.

Father at war

My father was a very lucky man. He set off with the Border Regiment in World War I by boat from Liverpool. About six miles out into the Irish Sea the ship hit a mine and began to sink. The colonel major announced by megaphone that he wanted the utmost discipline when it was time to abandon ship and get into the lifeboats and liferafts - he did not want to lose a single man. When they arrived back in Liverpool without losing a single man as far as my father could remember, they had lost all their equipment, horses and dogs (the dogs were used for carrying messages). Nevertheless, they embarked again as soon as possible and set off a second time.

Uncles Billy, Fred and Harry were with my father. Uncle Harry stayed out in India and set up a printing business but the other three came home again.

My father worked in grandfather's printing works when the Second World War began. After about six months, the local police sergeant went into the works and said to him: "I'm afraid, Elleray, you will have to stop what you are doing." and handed him a permit. "This permit will get you a bus or taxi and then a train to Birmingham where you will have to look for lodgings. No-one can refuse you lodgings. Tell them that you are there for war work. If anyone refuses, go to the police and they will tell the people that they have to take in war workers. Then you will report to Wilmot and Bredan's factory."

Father went home and told my mother what had happened. She was quite shocked and upset; prospects looked bleak for her and the children. He said: "I have to abide by the law and go to Birmingham. Several other men are going too." Without any further ado, he went and packed his case. He caught a bus to Windermere and then a train to Birmingham.

He was amazed to see the devastation that bombing had done to Birmingham. He knocked at several houses and got lodgings with a pleasant couple. Then he went to Wilmot and Bredan's factory, an engineering company making parts for engineering company making parts for engines and guns. Having been at the factory for some months, one of the bosses spotted my father on the shop floor doing draughtsman-type things on a pad and asked if he could look at what my father was doing. He then asked what my father's job had been before going to do war work, and he replied that he was a printer in his father's works at Ambleside. The boss's reply was: "I think we can find you a job upstairs in the offices, Mr Middleton. You are wasted on the shop floor." Soon after that the factory was bombed and my father had to move to another branch.

He was bombed out of his lodgings more than once during the time he was in Birmingham. On one occasion the house he was staying in was very badly damaged. He succeeded in getting out of bed (he was fully dressed because of the possibility of having to go to an air-raid shelter at any time) from under the debris of what had been the roof of the house, and made his way to the room next door. He found the owners dead in bed.

There was destruction all along the street with burning vehicles and some of the houses on fire as well.

Sometimes my father had to join the air raid patrols and help in putting bodies or parts of bodies into bags after bombing raids or doodle bugs (flying bombs) had landed. I used to sit for many an hour with my father during the evenings. He would weep when telling me about the awful sights he had witnessed. His experience during World War I had been bad enough but he had found the Second World War to be worse.

— ooooo —

My mother Hilda. GM

My mother in her later years. GM

Chapter 10 **My mother's life on farms**

When my mother was 12 years old she was taken to the auction at Ulverston by her mother and father to be hired. The lady and gentleman from Witherslack Hall came towards her and asked: "You are for hire?" Her parents replied: "Yes, she is.", whereupon the lady and gentleman asked her if she could do house-work such as washing up, cleaning and making beds, as well as milk cows and plough with horses. They were satisfied with her answers because they gave her the hiring coin and asked where her tin box was with her clothes and the other things she needed. She went with them, climbing on to the seat behind them in their pony and trap. The master said to her: "You don't sit there, my lass. You sit on the draw board at the back." So they set off to Witherslack Hall.

My mother had to start work when she arrived there. She had to help on the farm as they had indicated, and also in the mansion when they had drinks parties – sometimes into the early hours of the morning. Quite often she would then fall asleep while milking the cows in the morning. The hall had a milk round and it was one of her jobs to deliver the milk. Another job was to wash the clothes and peg them out on the line in the field to dry.

One day the master and lady called all the staff into the hallway and asked each one of them separately to turn out their pockets, and asked if they knew where the lady's jewellery had gone. The staff were accused of taking the jewellery. Most of them were young like my mother and were very embarrassed. After this, the policeman was called. He went to each room and found nothing.

A few days later my mother was hanging the washing out in the field when she noticed a jay going into a tree with something shiny in its beak. She went and told the lady, who immediately got one of the men to get a ladder up the tree. He brought the contents of the nest down to the lady. Among them were the jewellery that had been missing. My mother had watched long enough to see the jay go in the bedroom window and out again. Most of the children working at the hall were removed by their parents.

Granddad and Grandma Park took my mother away from Witherslack Hall. She was not being fed properly, being expected to work on half an egg and half a rasher of bacon. Bread and dripping were there as well but the amount of bread was limited. When she complained and said that they had hens at home but never half an egg, the master said: "Aye, my lass, but you are not at home now."

One of my mother's sisters was hired about a year later to go to Witherslack Hall but decided not to go there after learning about the food. She went to Rydal Hall instead where two other sisters were already working.

At the age of 16 my mother went to work on a farm near Preston and stayed there for two years. Then she returned to Ulverston to be hired again, and went to the Lyth Valley Hotel (not the present building – it was on the other side of the road). It was very hard work, including working behind the bar serving beer, milking the cows, feeding the various animals, collecting eggs and doing the milk round. After about three years she decided it was time for a change.

My mother's next employment was on a farm at Millom. After a few years she had to leave it. Mr and Mrs McKnight died within three years of each other and Mr McKnight the brother was left on his own. With tears in his eyes, he said to mother: "I'm sorry, Hilda. I'm going to have to sell up. We will have to bring all the tools and machinery from the byres and huts on to the front field. All the animals: shire horses, pigs, cows, sheep, hens, ducks, geese, will have to be assembled. And the contents of the farmhouse too." It would be hard to bear; and he might go and live with his cousin.

Many of the farmers who went to the sale were suffering too because they were in similar situations of being widowed or having no family to take over the farms.

Mother had offers to go and work at various farms, including further up the coast. She worked at Cockermouth for a while and then at Cleator Moor for several months and used to sleep above the dairy in both places. It was very cold. Grandma gave her a paraffin lamp. She kept it on night and kept warm. To get extra warmth, she sewed two sheets together and filled them with sawdust. But she was not happy and decided to go back to Ulverston Auction to be hired again. She had reached the age of 22.

At the auction, the people for hire – some of them older than she was – stood in a row to be assessed. Farmers from the area and as far away as Grasmere, Ambleside, Kendal and Lancaster walked along the row. Mr Herbert Bennett was one of them. He asked my mother to roll up her sleeves so he could look at her arms. "There doesn't seem to be anything wrong with your arms." He then asked about her legs.

"No, there is nothing wrong with my legs." was her reply.

"Before I give you the coin before I seal your employment with me, have you got any impediments?"

"No," she said, "I have no impediments. I am just as I am."

"Where is your tin box with all your things in?" he asked. She told him it was by Mackereth's shop in the Market Square up the road from the auction.

“Right, my lass. I have several things to do in Ulverston and one or two calls to make before going back to Ambleside. You have to make your way to Lakeside by train and get the steamer from there up to Waterhead. I will pick you up at Waterhead and take you to Roundhill Farm up the Kirkstone Road.”

He explained that there had originally been two Roundhill Farms, and that the farmhouse at High Roundhill Farm had been burnt down some years earlier. He asked her if she had ever done any walling or shearing or other farm-type jobs. He told her that he had a milk round in Ambleside and that she might sometimes have to deliver the milk to the customers. Turnips, potatoes and cabbage were grown on the farm, and cream was made particularly for the local hotels. She said she had grown turnips and potatoes.

Roundhill Farm

When mother arrived at the farm, things were in quite a mess. The bedroom was light and airy but most of the things were dilapidated and in poor condition. The floor had straw, sawdust and hay on it. She tried the bed and decided she would not sleep well on it. She was not pleased with the chest of draws but the wardrobe was OK. The toilet was outside. Mr Bennett said he would find out about getting a toilet fitted indoors. He also said that if she liked to go down into Ambleside to Dixon's furniture shop near Mason's Corner, she could order a new bed and anything else that would make the bedroom more suitable for her - this included a covering for the floor. He would take the cart down to pick up what she had ordered.

“I can't expect you to work hard on the farm if you don't have a comfortable bed to sleep on.” He gave her some money and she went down into Ambleside and got some fresh food too. She went to the Miss Coffees in North Road who said that he would be quite a good man to work for, but he could get drunk particularly on auction days. He often went down on horseback because there were so many carts in Ambleside on such days. His horse could be seen regularly tied up outside the Unicorn public house (also in North Road). If he went to Ulverston, it was not unknown for him to be strapped to his cart and have a rug draped round him. His horse would then find its way back to Roundhill Farm some 20 miles away. Mother never knew what time he might be back.

Mother had to plough the fields and sometimes sow corn, barley and wheat, and plant turnips, sugar beet and vegetables. Another job was to scythe bracken, and gather it on to sledges for dragging to the farm for bedding for the animals. Yet another job was to snag the turnips (cut off their tops) and cart them to the store. The sheep were then allowed into the field to eat the tops

Soon after mother started working at Roundhill Farm, Mr Bennett took her up the Kirkstone road to the inn at the top, saying that he farmed all the land up to the top of the fell. A little astonished, she asked if she was expected to go up there. He replied that his 10 dogs did most of the work with the sheep. Mother was not pleased with the dogs' living conditions and they were improved.

A view from Roundhill Farm.

She also worked in the farmhouse, in effect as housekeeper and cook; she baked and made bread. Mr Bennett said he liked a good meal on the table in front of him. In some of the farmhouses, for example at Roundhill Farm, they had bracken and rushes on the floor. One of the farmers was named Moses Jackson.

Mother was left to put the farm manure out in heaps in the fields and then spread it out with a fork. Later the farmer would get basic slag. It had to be collected from the lime kiln and be kept covered until it was in the field otherwise it would bubble up.

An occasional job was wall gapping. When the walls fell down the gaps had to be filled to keep the sheep and cows in the fields, on Sundays if necessary. One particular Sunday she was repairing a wall and the local vicar and his wife were walking up Kirkstone Road. Seeing her busy, he said to her: "You should not be walling on a Sunday, Hilda. It is the sabbath." She replied: "It is the only time I have spare to do these odd jobs. You should know a farm is a busy place in summer, and, after all, you work on a Sunday, sir."

In the autumn when they were harvesting the wheat, oats and barley, my mother used to go down to Gibson's Mill which was in North Road. Before setting off, she had to put leather shoes on the shire horses to stop them from slipping on the steep road. Sometimes there were two carts, one behind the other. It was not unusual to set out between four and half past in the morning so that she was ahead of the other arrivals. And it was not unusual that she had to unload the carts herself at the mill. On arriving back at the farm up The Struggle, she had to remove all the horses' harness and leather shoes, and then take them back into the field after giving them a bucket of feed.

Milking began at a very early hour. After bringing the cows in and washing them, she would wheelbarrow turnips, mangles and sugar beet into the parlour and put them through the hand-operated shredder. The chopped up feed was put into buckets together with oats and barley for the cows to eat while they were being milked. After the milking was finished, the cows would be turned out into the field once again. The milk would go through the cooler and be put into urns with brass tops. Then it was time to harness the pony to take the milk and vegetables down to various parts of the town and hotels - before having her breakfast. Sometimes while doing the deliveries, a lady called Mrs Horrax would give her a sandwich and a cup of tea.

With some of the milk my mother would make butter.

They also had to go down to Horrax's Bobbin Mill at Stock Ghyll to get sawdust and shavings for putting down as bedding for the horses, cows and young stock. Sometimes she had to go further to other mills, maybe to Skelwith Bridge or to Hawkshead, or the mill at Finsthwaite.

It was a very busy time in spring, especially at lambing time going round the sheep and checking that they and the lambs were alright. Being up all night happened from time to time; being a 'midwife' was a common task.

--- ooooo ---

Four views of the yard.

Chapter 11 **Chickens in the yard, and mending a bucket**

Captain Pickup came up to the yard at the end of Park Street one day with a chimney pot under his arm to put on our chimney (it was still there until recently). My mother was hanging some washing on the line in the yard. She decided to pluck up courage and ask him if she could keep some chickens in the yard. He said she could, and suggested that she get herself a small shed and put it in the corner of the yard. When she asked about putting a fence up to keep them in, he said no but let them roam free because there was plenty of grass in the yard.

She got some orange boxes from the co-op shop and made a small hen-house. She then went to Tinny Martin's for some felt and covered it to make it watertight, and some netting to put over the little door to keep them in at night – and cats and foxes out! The chickens came from Mr Stott who ran the fish and chip shop. She asked him if he had any chickens to spare when buying fish and chips.

The neighbours were kind and helped feed the chickens; in return we gave the neighbours fresh eggs.

Some time later, my mother did not say when, one of the hens became broody and stayed on a nest. She sent one of us to the grocer for a dozen eggs which she put under the hen. Then she told my father what she had done.

"You don't know whether they are fertile, especially when they have Canada stamped on them." said my father. "They won't hatch if they aren't."

"They have two chances." said my mother. "They will or they won't."

About three weeks passed. Mother noticed that something had happened and looked carefully under the hen. She called my father, who happened to be home from his war work in Birmingham. He was amazed because all twelve eggs had hatched into black chicks. The brood was eleven pullets and one cockerel. Father said he would make up a small pen for the hen and her chicks. The cockerel grew to become a magnificent bird with a large red comb and red wattles.

John Parsons came into the yard delivering milk. He also had a cockerel at that time. He saw the magnificent bird in the yard and told us that, if birds from the same clutch breed, the chicks would be deformed. So the cockerels were swapped.

It was not long after that that I started to help John on his farm. I asked him one day if there was anywhere on his land that I could keep my hens. He said I could use the hog house if I wanted to, and put up a shed in Cicely Woods as well. I acquired a big hut and Robin Ives helped me put it up. It was grand – big enough to keep the chickens indoors during wet weather.

And then John Parsons and I had a disagreement. I was working for Mr Fielding at the time and told him what had happened. He allowed me to put the hut in his field until I had my own field at Castlefield in Ambleside.

When my mother kept the chickens in the yard, she had a special bucket for their food; it was just right for the job As time went by the bottom of it got worse and worse until the bucket needed repairing or replacing. She decided on buying a new one and sent me to Tinny Martin's to buy it.

"What's wrong with the old one?" asked Mr Martin. "Go and get it and I will see if I can repair it as new buckets are quite expensive."

I returned to the shop with the bucket which he put on a machine. This could be made to rotate by means of a foot pedal. He started the machine going round and tapped the rim with a small hammer until the rim came off. Changing tools he then cut round the bottom of the bucket so that most of the bottom was cut out. Beside him was a collection of round pieces of tin in many sizes. He selected one and placed it in the bottom of the bucket. Then he lit a small gas jet and began heating a soldering iron. The next stage was rotating the bucket and applying the solder as the bucket went round. When that was done, he told me to take the bucket over to the other side of the shop and put some water in it to see if it leaked. It did not.

Mother was highly delighted when I told her how much it had cost.

"A shilling (5p)." Mr Martin had said. "That has saved your mother a bit because a new bucket is three and a tanner. (17½p)"

--- ooooo ---

Chapter 12 **A sandboat tragedy, and road mending**

The local council had a sandboat which was moored on Mr MacIver's land behind where the shelter is in Borrans Park at Waterhead. The boat was used daily when the weather was not too bad to collect sand from the mouth of the River Rothay.

One day it was overloaded and it sank. Several local men lost their lives; most of them could not swim. The bell of Ambleside church was tolled as a mark of respect.

The boat was not used again by the council but the Pattinson firm of builders in Bowness-on-Windermere did do so for a while.

When the roads were repaired in Ambleside by the local council, the foreman was Jack Fisher and he had several local men working for him: Jack Prickett who used to drive the steamroller, and Bill Clark, Mr Capstick, Ham Nicholson, as well as Bob Dixon, Bill Walker and Dan Tyson. If you told Jack Fisher there was a hole in the road, his response was that it would be seen to promptly. If a manhole was loose, it would be similarly dealt with.

There were several places on the roadsides where the council used to store the materials to repair the roads before they were tarmaced. They were called Sammel Holes. One was where the Nat West Bank is now, another was near Lowfold, and another opposite the entrance to Rydal Farm on the way to Grasmere. There were many others on the way to Grasmere and Windermere.

It used to amaze me as a boy watching to see how the steamroller went up Kirkstone Road. The roadmen would spread tar on the road and then a layer of chippings. These were rolled in by the steamroller. Two of the men kept close to the machine. Each of them had a long pole with a block of wood on the end which they put under the back 'wheels' to stop the steamroller from rolling unintentionally down the hill.

--- ooooo ---

Ethel Johnson's memorial in St Mary's Churchyard.
It stands about 19 inches (48cm) high.

Chapter 13 **Ethel Johnson, the lady for the birds**

One of our local doctors was named Johnson. He lived in a large house opposite the White Lion Hotel and used the sitting room for his surgery; two sisters, the Miss Simons, were the housekeepers. (The building was demolished many years ago to become the post office. That building has also been demolished. The present building has become a supermarket.) He had a sister called Ethel.

She used to go by the school almost every day, carrying a basket or sometimes two. When I was in the Infant School in Miss MacKenzie's class we wondered what was in the baskets. Ethel was friendly and used to talk to us through the railings.

"You must look after the little birds." she used to tell us.

One day we had the courage to ask her what was in the baskets. She told us that she went to the local bakers and grocers shops for stale bread and for anything else that she could feed to the birds in the park and under Loughrigg.

On another occasion she told us:
"One day when I have left this world, I will still look after the little birds."

As children, this mystified us and we laughed about it, thinking it was very amusing that she could do something after she was dead. But many years later I discovered in the churchyard at St Mary's in Ambleside that her memorial was made to catch water for the birds, as shown in the photograph opposite. So she does indeed still look after the birds but in a different way.

--- ooooo ---

Chapter 14 **Uncle Bill, Aunt Agnes and two fires**

Uncle Bill and Aunt Agnes had been to market day at Ulverston and did not know of what had been happening to their home in Finsthwaite until they were nearly back there. A fire had destroyed it; nothing could have been done to save it. Apparently, a thunderstorm had occurred during the day and the building had been struck by lightening.

They bought a shop with an adjoining house in Ulverston and ran the business for some years. There was an internal door which connected between the shop and the house. I do not remember what caused Uncle Bill's death but aunty closed the shop when he died, locked the connecting door, and lived in the house for many more years.

One night we had all settled down and gone to bed when a knock came at our door. It was the police. They wanted us to go to Ulverston. Aunt Agnes had fallen into the fire and burnt the side of her head. When we arrived at her home the doctor was there and he was trying to persuade her that she needed to go to hospital for treatment to her wound.

Aunt Agnes said: “All I need is brown paper and goose grease.”

My mother tried to talk to her but she was quite obstinate.

Aunt Agnes said: “I'm not going to hospital. You will not get a penny from my will if you send me to hospital.” However, my mother finally persuaded her and they took her to Ulverston Cottage Hospital. In time her head got better. We used to go quite frequently to see her.

She lived for a fair while afterwards and went to live in a residential home as she seemed unable to look after herself properly.

When Aunt Agnes died and the funeral was over, my mother received a letter from the solicitor at Ulverston with a cheque for a headstone at Finsthwaite Church. Having eventually got a headstone completed, we took it down to the church. We went to the vicarage and found a note on the door to say that the vicar was away on holiday, and to go to the verger with any enquiries. The verger was in fact away for that day. So we laid the stone on the grave.

One week later we received an unpleasant letter from the vicar saying we had no permission to put the stone on the grave. He was going to throw it under the hedge.

Mother said to me: "Come on. Let's go down to Finsthwaite and sort the vicar out about this." When we arrived at Finsthwaite Church she met the vicar and told him it was not a very Christian way for a vicar to act, especially since Aunt Agnes had left most of her money to the church. After further discussion, the stone was placed on the grave.

St Peter's Church, Finsthwaite

With Aunt Agnes having died, it was time to clear the property where she and Uncle Bill had lived. The lock of the connecting door to the shop still had the key in it. Neither the key nor the lock offered any resistance because they were so rusty. We found that nothing in the shop had been touched since it had been closed so many years earlier. The pre-decimal money was still in the till. We had to be careful moving about because woodworm had been able to infest the floors and the furniture. A chair fell into a heap when I touched it. A distantly-related cousin arrived while the property was being cleared. We kept very little of its contents but I do remember keeping a bowl and jug from one of the bedrooms.

A twist in this story is that the widow of the man who had been Uncle Frank's boss bought the land with the home destroyed by fire and had a new home built there for herself.

--- ooooo ---

Chapter 15 **Local old men, and building firms**

I used to sit with local old men at the cross and on the window ledge of Boots the chemist: Tom Armer, Jack Pearce, Ham Nicholson, Brate Black, and the Blaylock brothers. (The building that was Boots is now the Post Office and Tourist Information Centre.) The old men told me about young men liking to get jobs at Newton's Quarry because they were well paid and well looked after. They had good stone buildings to have their meals in whereas most of the quarries had just shelters. Sometimes I used to watch Tom Newton working the stone in his yard in Compston Road as he fashioned the different pieces to the shape and size required. I found watching craftsmen very useful.

Sitting on the window ledge at Boots came to an end when metal bars with spikes were fitted to the sills. But we did not move far – just next door to the windowsill at Mackereth's shop.

When the Herds came to Ambleside, Mr Herd bought the property called Rattlegill which was two rows of houses. They were pulled down and the Central Buildings took their place. On the corner next to North Road was Mr Herd's chemist shop (later this became Boots). To the left of it was a Mackereth shop, then Bruce Squire's fishing tackle shop and a Mackereth toy shop. Next was Bob Bones' fruit shop and then Wilf Nicholson's which became Anoraks in Profusion. Further along were Crossland and Backhouse's fishmonger and game business, and finally Rushforth's sweet and tobacco shop. This last one is now the newsagent Whittaker's.

Where the Spar shop is in Compston Road was built when father was a boy, originally as houses.

Bob Bones grew fruit and vegetables a garden which extended for most of the way from Millans Park to the top of Compston Road, including where the cinema is. He went round the town selling his produce. Benson Harrison owned the garden; he eventually moved into one of Mr Herd's shops and was there nearly a lifetime.

When the Mackereth's first came to Ambleside they sold their wares close to Stock Ghyll where the Rock Shop is now in North Road.

Mr Palfreyman's garden and the area in front of the Salutation Hotel used to be an open space which was used from time to time as a fairground.

Where the fire station is now on Rydal Road used to be allotments. There were allotments down the other side of Stoney Lane too.

Going further down Stoney Lane leads to Miller Bridge (1888), Pelter Bridge, and Rothay Bridge. There was so much water in the big flood of 1888 that the Rothay Bridge was washed away. Rothay Park and the infant school were flooded. It was one of the worst floods that my father told me about.

The gatepost in Millans Park of Bob Bones' garden.
The hinges for the gate are on the far side of the post.

Jacksons were local builders too. My father recalled Mr Jackson being known by the nickname Jibbie.

Jackson's Yard was a local stonemason's yard. Mr Jackson was the builder of most of Millans Park, and of many other properties. Much is said and written about poets, painters and writers in the Lake District but there is little mention of the people who actually constructed the Ambleside we see today. Another local firm was the Backhouse Builders.

Henry Jennings was another builder. He took over Jibbie Jackson's yard until the tragedy of losing his only son who was just 14 years old. The accident was caused by workers playing a prank on the son. They pinned up his lunch bag on a high beam. When he tried to get it he put his arm through the gap in a belt driving the machinery and became entangled by the belt. It pulled him up to the top and he was killed - a terrible sight for his parents.

The yard was closed until the Second World War started. The council took it over for storing waste paper.

Jibbie Jackson lived on Wansfell Road. Most of the houses there were built by him. The road used to be called Red Bottoms because of the red sammel down there which was used for filling holes in the road before tarmac came into use. The road was also Jibbie's private road. Tradesmen who went down the road had to pay a toll, so they waited until they had many items to deliver and paid as infrequently as possible. The Slack, Fairview Road and Nook Lane were other roads on which tolls were paid during my grandfather's days.

My father, coming home for his midday meal one day, was outside the Crossland and Backhouse shop as were the proprietors - Mr Backhouse with his thumbs in his braces - when Mr McAdam from the council came along. He gestured towards the fish and game on open display. New regulations meant that in future the shop window would have to be closed. No fish on display could be reached from the pavement. Likewise, no game could be hung on the bar outside the shop. Everything would have to be displayed inside the shop.

Mr Backhouse turned to Mr Crossland and said that, if that was the case, it was time to close the business. Mr McAdam said that his wife came to do business with them, to which Mr Backhouse said she would have to go elsewhere.

The business was indeed closed down. These particular premises have been the Fred Holdsworth bookshop for many years now.

--- ooooo ---

An old postcard

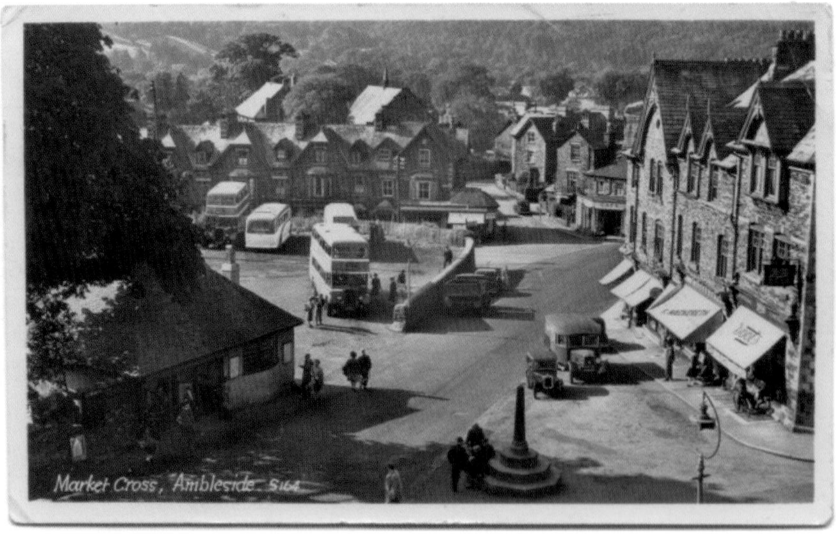

A postcard from my collection showing the bus station at the top of Compston Road, the Market Cross, and the Central Buildings on the right.

Chapter 16 **Roses and post offices**

Mr Golding was the first postmaster when the post office was opened at the corner of Millans Park and Vicarage Road, and was still the postmaster when he retired. (The building was specifically built as a post office. It is now the Walnut fish and chip shop and the Chocolate Bar.) His hobby was growing roses and his garden was close by in Compston Road. Climbers, ramblers, floribundas and hybrid tees were all among his collection. The scent from them could be detected along much of Compston Road during the summer. The garden is now also very different - it is the Tagore Restaurant.

His home was between the Whittans and the Wilsons in what was known locally as the bottom row in Millans Park. I remember him saying to Miss Elliott, who also lived on the row, that he had bred a new red rose which he would call Miss Elliott and give her to plant in her own garden during the autumn. Mrs Jackson and Mrs Christopherson were among the other people to receive roses for planting. Millans Park used to be one of the best places in Ambleside for roses because of the number that Mr Golding gave away.

One of my great aunts worked at the first post office which was in Rydal Road during the 1880s. This building is now occupied by Dodd's Cafe.

--- ooooo ---

Close examination of the postcard reveals:

Two people sitting on the windowsill of Boots, at the righthand edge of the picture, with someone sitting on a bicycle in front of them.

Two doubledecker buses displaying the route number 555, the one nearer the camera displaying Kendal and the other one Ambleside. The 555 service still operates today.

From the road markings and the manner in which vehicles are parked, the roads were two-way at that time. There is a signpost pointing to the left down Compston Road to Coniston and Langdale.

A tinted photograph from my school days. GM

Chapter 17 **Piglets and a circus**

I was coming home from school one day at the age of about ten when a man called Albert Faulkner stopped in Compston Road and said: "Do you want to go to Cockermouth with me and collect some piglets?" I said I would like to go but I would have to ask my parents first. So I went home and asked if I could go; my Dad said: "Aye, you'll be alright with Albert."

We set off in an old van which had been the County Stores van. We proceeded along Rydal Road and were just past the entrance to Rydal Farm when some of the boards in the back of the van fell into the road. Albert said: "Jump out, lad, and pick them up. Don't worry about them falling out when the piglets are in. The weight of the piglets will stop the boards moving. We may have to do something with the boards before we load the piglets." The boards fell out again before we arrived at Cockermouth. Eventually, we did arrive at the farm. Albert said: "Thou stay there while I do the deal with the farmer." The farmer met him at the door and they went inside.

Albert came out a bit later with the farmer and they both had a glass in their hand. They put the glasses down and Albert backed up the van to the barn.

We then loaded the piglets, 30 of them, and shut the doors on them. I wanted to sit in with them but Albert said I had better sit in front where I sat before. We set off for Ambleside after saying goodbye to the farmer and his family.

Everything went well until we got to Thirlmere. The road was still very narrow then and had not been widened. Along came some circus wagons going in the opposite direction. Albert said: "I will have to get well into the side to let these wagons go by."

What we did not know was that, while the wagons squeezed by, a large stone had somehow dislodged itself and dropped in between the front and rear wheels of the van on my side. We set off again, only for the back wheel to ride joltingly over the stone. All of the boards in the back of the van slipped, the doors opened, and all the piglets made their escape on to the road.

We tried desperately to catch them. It was quite a job. Cars were held up both ways. After some time, people in the cars who had car rugs helped to catch the piglets. Even so, it took a while to collect them all. If we had not have had that help, I do not know what we would have done.

There were no more mishaps before we arrived back in Ambleside.

--- ooooo ---

Features of Ambleside

This sign stands at the junction of Compston Road, Millans Park and Vicarage Road. The ring at the top displays Ambleside U.D.C.

Ambleside Urban District Council ceased to exist when I was a small boy.

This sign stands on the approach to Rothay Bridge on the road from Hawkshead and Coniston.

It displays the initials A.U.D.C.

Chapter 18 **No more Lancashire Evening Post**

Delivering newspapers around Ambleside for Mr Ernest Bennett involved meeting many people and a lengthy walk each time. Now and again the prices went up.

On one such occasion I was asked to tell Miss Hart, who lived on Low Gale, that the price of the Lancashire Evening Post had increased from 2d to 2½d (up to 1p in modern currency). Miss Hart had been a music and dance teacher at the Charlotte Mason College before retiring.

When I arrived at the door I pulled the bell chord and heard the bell ring at some distance in the house. A dog rushed to the door and barked. I waited. The dog was retrieved and taken to a back room. Then I heard a high-level bolt being withdrawn on the inside of the door. A second, lower, bolt was with-drawn, and then a third. A fourth bolt was with-drawn, and then a fifth at the bottom of the door. But the door did not open. A mortice lock was unlocked, followed by a second mortice lock. Finally, a night latch was unlocked and the door opened, squeaking as it did so.

"Well, boy, what do you want?" was the greeting from the lady inside.

"Mr Bennett has asked me to tell you, madam, that the price of the Lancashire Evening Post has gone up from tuppence to tuppence ha'penny from last week."

"I suppose you want the money for last week."

Pulling herself up to full stature, she said: "Here is the money for last week. And please tell Mr Bennett that I shall no longer require the Lancashire Evening Post."

The door was closed, the locks were locked, the five bolts were slid back into their closed positions, and I continued on my round.

--- ooooo ---

Features of Ambleside

North Road is a two-way street but wide enough for only one vehicle for part of its length.

This road and Smithy Brow (Golden Rule Hill) were the main route through Ambleside until the section of Rydal Road in front of Bridge House was constructed.

This building (also in the photograph above) used to be Gibson's mill, where my mother brought cart loads of cereals for milling and my Aunt Coffees bought flour. The Unicorn public house is next door.

This view is from Stock Bridge where we used to wait for our Saturday pennies (page 20).

Chapter 19 **Groceries by Rolls, and other deliveries**

One of the regular features of my early life was the weekly delivery to the house of groceries. Mr Rose, who owned the Country Store in Ambleside, would sit on the chair just inside the front door and ask my mother for any variations on the usual order of flour, salt, butter, and other things. The order would be delivered in due course – by Rolls Royce! The total cost of the groceries was less than a pound.

On one occasion he said that the order would have to be for two weeks because the Rolls Royce would be off the road. The back part of the bodywork was going to be cut off and converted into a van so that there would be more room for the groceries.

Fruit and vegetables were brought round by Nellie Hodgson. John Parsons came round with milk, potatoes, eggs and cream. Joseph Perruzo came with his three-wheeler icecream cart and continued to do so when he bought a more modern van. Marsh's lemonade van delivered soft drinks. Tea came from Rington's tea man.

And a fishmonger used to come with his horse and cart from Flookburgh, a distance of about 20 miles. The cart looked much like a ridge tent on wheels, with a sheet (tarpaulin) covering it. In the top part would be piles of cockles, mussels, and other shellfish. On a shelf underneath them would be a variety of fish. There was a small gutting space at the back of the cart where he would prepare the fish if the customers wanted him to. The local cats took no time at all in appearing whenever he arrived. The smell was too great for them to ignore it, and they were always ready to accept the heads and other unwanted bits.

Later he had an open-back van instead of the horse and cart.

Milkmen

Ambleside has had many milkmen. In addition to John Parsons already mentioned, each of the following people or farms had their own milk round: Rydal Farm, Roundhill Farm, Brow Head Farm, Morris Farm at Brathay, Bigland's farm at Halfway House, Nicholson's, The Grove Farm, Nab Farm at Rydal, John Benson from Skelwith Fold, Town End dairy farm which for a while had both a horse and cart and a van, Nook End Farm, two or three farms at Grasmere, Brate Black from Lowfold Farm, Stevenson's under Loughrigg, Jim Chapman's farm, the Woodhouse's at Low Wray Farm, and Lanty Constable's Fisherbeck Farm.

--- ooooo ---

The home on Old Lake Road of Ab Routledge and his wife.

This building on Lake Road used to be Ab Routledge's woodshed.

Chapter 20 **Ab Routledge**

When I was a lad about 11 years old, Ab Routledge, who lived on Old Lake Road, used to come into the yard selling sacks of logs at one and thrupence (about 6p) each. Mother always had at least two.

To me he was an old man. Getting the sacks off the cart was very difficult for him because of the arthritis in his back, legs and hands. And it was not easy for him to carry them to the house. One day mother said I had better go and give him a hand. He was pleased that I did.

Later, mother said that I could help him deliver the sacks around the town. So I did. This involved loading the cart with the sacks of logs at his woodshed and then delivering them. Each load went to a different part of Ambleside. At the end of the day, the chestnut pony that pulled the cart was taken from Ab's home to the field across Lake Road next to the Log House Restaurant.

After a while Ab asked me to go with him to collect the wood for the logs from places such as Grasmere, Hawkshead and Sawrey (between Hawkshead and Ferry House). I used to help him saw them into the logs and to burn the bits and pieces he could not sell. Sometimes a lad called Bill Grundy also helped us. People who allowed Ab to take boughs of the trees included the two Dixon brothers who owned the mill at Sawrey.

Ab kept pigs where the garage is in the lower photograph, and let Brate Black keep half a dozen cows in the top part of the building where the wood was stored. Sometimes Brate was milking his cows (by hand) while Ab and I were busy sawing wood just a few feet away.

--- ooooo ---

Features of Ambleside

Bridge Street still has the cobbles and flagstones from the days of the horse and cart.

The top end at North Road.

The bottom end at Rydal Road.

Chapter 21 **Paper and rags, and a big fire**

For the war effort (Second World War) my schoolteacher Mrs Ashley said to us in class one day that it would be good to collect waste paper, rags and cardboard. So I used to go round the shops in Ambleside with an old pram made into a bogey (I replaced the baby part of the pram with a wooden box).

Sometimes it was necessary to go down into the cellars of the shops to bring things out. They included clothes and hats. Mr Bland's hat shop was next door to the Co-op in Compston Road, and there could be quite a lot to be taken away from there.

The depot for the waste paper was initially in Back Compston (Compston Street), part of Mr Jennings' property. Mr Jack Prickett was in charge; he put the waste through a press.

We were all at school one day when we heard the fire siren and we found out that the fire was just up the road at the waste paper depot where Millans Court is now. The school master took us all to see the fire. It destroyed the depot. We were nearly scorched by the heat and we saw the roof cave in. The fire crew had a difficult job. The officer was Jack Fisher. The Prickett brothers, Bill Hindmoor, Albert Loughland, Billy and Fudge Nicholson, Dan Tyson and a member of the Dawson family were among the crew.

--- ooooo ---

The Gables Hotel.

Chapter 22 **Johnny Bell and Appleby Horse Fair**

Johnny Bell had a riding school. He owned The Gables near the parish church. He hired out the horses and ponies, and his daughter Jean often took American servicemen out to the valleys such as at Langdale and Kirkstone. The servicemen were stationed at Burton Wood during the Second World War.

When I was 12 years old I used to take the ponies to the field, sometimes down Stoney Lane to the field at the bottom and sometimes across the beck where the fire station is. A local name for the beck was Butchers Beck. Large numbers of worn-out horses and ponies used to be killed there on its banks.

One day, Johnny said to me: “Would you like to go to Appleby Horse Fair? I am going to buy some horses. If you would like to come with me, we will set off at 4 o'clock in the morning. You must ask your parents if it is alright for you to go.”

I did, and they said I could go.

So we set off for the fair and picked up a Mr Pearson on the road to Crook who had arranged to go with Johnny.

We arrived at the fair. Johnny said to me: “Right, George. You go and have a look round for a spell while I go and look at the horses. Go and have a look at the caravans, too. Then come back in a couple of hours or so and we will have something to eat.”

I went and looked at the caravans. Sitting outside on of them was a couple. “Now, lad, would you like a cup of tea?”

I said: “Yes please, that would be grand.”

They gave me a cup of tea in a bakelite cup, and the gypsy man said: “Would you like a piece of prairie chicken and brown bread?”

“Yes please.” So they gave me a piece of prairie chicken and some lovely brown bread.

Then they asked if I would like to look inside the caravan. I said I would, and found it was beautifully done out and had a fireplace at the far end. I thanked them for giving me the tea, prairie chicken and bread, and went to look at other caravans. It was most interesting to watch some of the owners who were baking bread in the ground.

After I had had a good look round, I went back to where Johnny had the pony and trap. He had bought a couple of horses. We had something to eat and drink, and then set off back to Ambleside. It rained nearly all the way. He asked me how I liked the gypsy caravans. I said they were absolutely beautiful. And I told him about how the couple had given me a cup of tea and prairie chicken with brown bread. He burst out laughing. "Do you know what thou's eaten? You have eaten hedgehog! It won't do you any harm. It's what a lot of working men used to have to eat as well as gypsies."

Another thing I did at about the age of 12 was to go with Johnny to Greta Gate Farm on the coast near Broughton to take some of his horses there for the winter. The climate was milder than at Ambleside. On other occasions we would take horses north to a coastal farm near Maryport. He knew the people there very well. When we brought the horses back in the spring we would bring sacks of oats and other feedstuffs as well for the horses.

--- ooooo ---

Features of Ambleside

Stock Ghyll beside the fire station.

Chippy Davis and the Russian man with the performing bears slept on benches here.

This part was also known as Butchers Beck.

Chapter 23 **Social event at Hawkshead**

I enjoyed going to social events from a young age.

News spread of a forthcoming event in Hawkshead, and I decided that I would like to go to it. So I did, with a friend John Grundy who lived at Pull Wyke on the way to Hawkshead.

There was quite a gathering of people when we got there, and I recognised many of them.

I was recognised too by one particular lady through my family connection with grandfather's printing business. She came over to me and told me that I was not welcome. The event, she said, was for people local to Hawkshead, Near Sawrey and Far Sawrey, not for people from Ambleside. She got hold of me by the left ear and took me out of the door to the gate so that I did not stay any longer.

Her last words were: "Be gone if you do not want a taste of this." and showed me the whip that I knew she invariably carried inside her cape.

The lady was Mrs Heelis, Beatrix Potter.

I set off home.

But I had not gone very far when I met Jack Pooley and his family going the other way. He asked me where I was going so I told him, and why. His response was that I should turn round and join them. He would see to it that I was not turned away again. He did indeed tell Mrs Heelis that he had invited me to the event.

--- ooooo ---

Features of Ambleside

In Old Lake Road. The buffer in the middle of this picture dates from the days of the horse and cart. Its purpose was to prevent cart wheels from damaging the wall by forcing them away from the wall.

Three much smaller buffers can be seen when standing outside the Queen's Hotel: one is to the right at the top of The Slack; the other two are across the road, one at the foot of the steps of the Market Hall and the other at the corner of the building across the short road to the left of the Market Hall.

The site in North Road of Ambleside's stocks, beside Stock Ghyll.

Chapter 24 **Hound dogs**

Several men in Ambleside had a hobby of keeping hound dogs.

Alf Bigland stopped me in the street one day and said: "Now, me lad. Do you want to earn yourself half a crown?" (12½p)

"Will you walk up to the Grove and then go up on the fell and up the bank at the Skelghyll Woods? I will go with you the first time to show you where I want you to go, and you come down Strawberry Bank where Miss Bell lived and at the back of the private house Wansfell, and across the top of Lanty Constable's field, and come out by Fisherbeck Car Park and then up Old Lake Road and then into Low Gale and Back Yam, to my house in the 55 Steps."

We went to his backyard where he had a smelly old bucket which had rags soaked in human urine and aniseed in it.

"We will have something to eat before we start." he said.

The rags were put in a sack which we dragged along. We took the bucket too to resoak the rags. I did this for a few years for half a crown each time.

What the sack was for was to leave a scent trail for the hound dogs. He had several hound dogs and some of them were puppies. Sometimes I had to go back round where I had laid the trail because, if the hound dogs found a dead sheep, they would feast on it. I would have to put them on a lead to get them away from it and take them back home.

From doing that I used to do odd jobs for him and for his brother who lived at Halfway House.

Every now and then when I got back, his wife Mrs Bigland would give me some homemade lemonade with a big chunk of fruit cake or a cup of tea with a sandwich.

--- ooooo ---

The former Methodist Church and Hall in Ambleside.

It is now Wesley Court, having been converted into homes for local people.

Chapter 25 **The Middleton 'family' grows**

Sergeant Major Carnes was stationed with an Irish tank regiment at Grasmere during the Second World War. His wife was heavily pregnant but had nowhere to live. He had called everywhere in Grasmere but no-one would take his wife in to live with them.

They came to Ambleside one day and joined a group of people who were standing in the open space in front of the Methodist Church. These people had been evacuated from their homes to the peace of the Lake District. Miss Routledge, a school-teacher, spoke to the sergeant major and his wife and told them that she thought Mrs Middleton would be able to help in some way.

There was a knock at our door.

"See who it is, George, please."

I opened it to find three people standing outside.

I went and told mother that it was Miss Routledge the schoolteacher, a lady with a very big tummy, and a man in uniform.

"Ask them in, will you?"

When they had come in and sat down, it did not take the man and woman long to explain the rather desperate circumstances they were in.

Mother said that she could not turn the wife away; she could stay with us.

The baby, a girl, was born three weeks later. The midwife had been called but was delayed so much that there was nothing for her to do when she arrived. The new mum was so pleased with her baby and that there had been no complications that she said she had to name the baby Hilda after mother.

A young woman was looking for somewhere to live while expecting a baby. She had knocked on many doors before she knocking on ours. Mother invited her in and listened to what she had to say. Mother then promptly said she could stay with us; some of us children could sleep in the attic to make space for her. I do not remember her name.

The baby was born and named Michael, and the young woman took a job at Dodd's Cafe to earn some money to help pay her way. She met a man named Bill Pointer during the course of her work. He was a bus conductor and went to the cafe for some of his breaks. They became good friends and, after going out together for several months, he told my mother that he had asked the lady to marry him. Mother arranged for the wedding car to be a Rolls Royce.

My partner Anne and I still meet Michael from time to time.

Dodd's Cafe no longer includes the premises on the corner of Rydal Road, but is still in business next door.

--- ooooo ---

Chapter 26 **Captain Poole**

During the Second World War a gentleman by the name of Captain Poole came to live in Ambleside. He bought Sweden House, a mansion in Sweden Bridge Lane which was once owned by a Miss Brown. The house has been converted into flats and the garages into houses. The kitchen garden, the wood and the front lawns have all been built on too. Captain Poole purchased houses in Millans Park and elsewhere in Ambleside. He also bought Jackson's Yard, which is now Millans Court, and later let the Fletcher family use the stables which were there.

When he came to Ambleside, Captain Poole brought his staff with him. There were housekeepers, the gardener Mr Hislop and his family and the chauffeur Mr Scott whom he held in high regard. Sadly, after three years or so, Captain Poole died. He left Mr Scott some property and his Rolls-Royce. After a while, Mr Scott wanted something extra to do and applied for a taxi licence for the Rolls-Royce. We used to hire it to go to various events such as dances and hunt balls at Langdale, Troutbeck, Grasmere and elsewhere. It used to cost about 10 shillings (50p) each. Later still, Mr Scott became a bus conductor because he was not too busy with his taxi.

Mr Scott's son started a garage in Jackson's Yard when he came back home after the war. Mr Scott moved into Industrial House there. Previously, it had been the offices for Jennings Builders. It was from Mr Scott that I bought a van, for £1,000. He had several clever mechanics including Morris Glaister and Peter Dugdale, a member of a local family, and owned Walker's garage too.

--- ooooo ---

The famous Bridge House in Ambleside.

I watched Kurt several times sitting at his easel creating paintings of this building.

It has just two rooms. The outside dimensions of the building are approximately 9 feet wide and 9 feet from front to back (2.7m by 2.7m) ignoring the steps beside the front door.

Blow Fat Cunningworth had a shoe repair business here for a while (he repaired shoes for my father when he was a boy). At bedtime, Blow Fat could be seen mounting the steps carrying a lighted candle and wearing a bobble hat.

Kurt Schwitter's stool.

Chapter 27 **Kurt Schwitters**

The schoolmaster Harry Bickerstaff used to take school groups for walks up on to Loughrigg. We used to collect newts and lizards and also frog spawn for putting in glass urns on the windowsills in the school.

We went up Loughrigg one day. Up there was the artist Kurt Schwitters who was living in a tent. He painted pictures where he was. Mr Bickerstaff said to him that it was no place for him to be. "I can find you a room at our house in Millans Park." After school had finished, Mr Bickerstaff went up Loughrigg again and persuaded Kurt to come down to their house. Kurt said he had no money and he would pay them with some pictures.

He moved in with the Bickerstaffs and lived there until Mrs Bickerstaff started having a family. Then he had to move out but Mr Bickerstaff told him not to worry because a good friend Charles Creighton had said he could move just a few doors along the road to live with him. Kurt used to visit where Charles had his blacksmith shop in The Slack and sharpened mowers (these premises are now a fish and chip shop). As a boy I used to go there myself and often saw Kurt sitting by his easel and painting. Another place he went to was to sit by Flo Lupton's antique shop on Rydal Road (now the ice cream shop next to the Apple Pie). I also sat on the wall closeby at Bridge House sometimes to watch him there. Yet other places were the cellar of Charles' house, out at Langdale, and at Waterhead. Kurt used to walk out to Langdale in his old gaberdine coat which was marked with paint and with much rust from squeezing between the iron work in Charles' blacksmith shop.

I still have the stool that Kurt used to sit on. When Flo Lupton closed the business down she asked me if there was anything in her shop that I would like. I chose the stool and three toby jugs. Flo closed down her other shop in Church Street at the same time.

The toby jugs got broken but not the stool.

I remember the night some 20 years or more after Kurt died that his remains were exhumed at the request of his family, who took them to Germany for burial there.

The memorial to Kurt Schwitters in St Mary's Churchyard.

--- ooooo ---

The lower grounds of Charlotte Mason College, now part of the University of Cumbria, opposite Stoney Lane.

Chapter 28 **My first job**

I mentioned in chapter 3 that I started work at Charlotte Mason College when I left school. I was under the supervision of the head gardener Mr Flitters, for £1 a week. But it was not only gardening. We had to go to the various buildings including Springfield, Fairfield, and the annex to stoke the boilers, to the cellars check the shoes and wellingtons to see if they were clean and not too worn (and take them to the principal for checking if necessary), clean out the pigs every morning, clean out the duck hut and hen house, collect any eggs that had been laid and take them to the kitchen, and go to the kitchen gardens and collect the vegetables the chef wanted, such as cabbage, cauliflower, potatoes, beetroot, carrots, turnips, and lettuce.

We used to have our morning break in the potting shed. There we were told what jobs we would be doing for the rest of the day such as mowing the lawns, sweeping the driveways, potting up plants, weeding the flower beds, collecting fruit from the trees and filbert and hazel nuts, or tending the vegetable garden. Other jobs included taking the handcart to collect the swill (unwanted food from local businesses and such things as potato peelings) for the pigs. This was boiled and then mixed with meal for feeding to them. Their bedding had to be checked. The straw came from Mr Slack at Rydal Farm and John Parsons at Hawks Farm. A good part of the job was when we had to look after new piglets.

The college was almost self sufficient. They had to buy some things like sugar, flour and salt but they had their own animals to provide meat and milk. We used to go back on Saturdays to help kill the pigs or cut up a cow carcase. From the pigs we made hams, bacon, sausages, poloni, gammon and brawn. Nothing was wasted; even the intestines were cleaned, washed, sterilised and used for making sausages.

We were not allowed to walk on the lawns after they had been cut. Nor were the children. If we were seen on the lawns, Mr Flitters would be told and we would be reprimanded by him. On one occasion I was told by Miss Trebenzie herself.

I went to a hunt ball at Coniston with a friend Fred Prickett. We missed the last bus home so we walked instead, a distance of about eight miles (about 13 km). Being tired the next morning I got up late. Consequently. I arrived late for work. Mr Flitters had already rebuked me once for being late. He looked at his watch and said: “What time do you call this? You are half an hour late. You can turn round and go home. You are sacked.”

And I was, on the spot.

--- ooooo ---

Milligan's nursery. GM

Situated on Borrans Road, the site is now a cul-de-sac with bungalows.

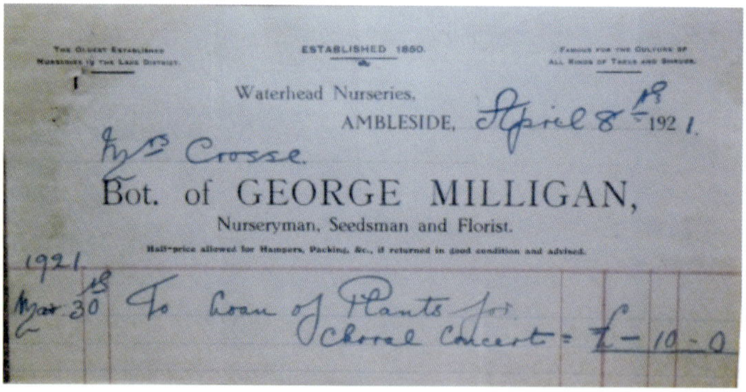

The Oldest Established Nurseries in the Lake District.

ESTABLISHED 1850.

Famous for the Culture of All Kinds of Trees and Shrubs.

Waterhead Nurseries,
AMBLESIDE, April 8th 1921.

Mrs Crosse

Bot. of GEORGE MILLIGAN,

Nurseryman, Seedsman and Florist.

Half-price allowed for Hampers, Packing, &c., if returned in good condition and advised.

1921 Mar	30th	To Loan of Plants for Choral Concert =	£	– 10	– 0

10s (£0.50) for the loan of plants for a concert in 1921.

Chapter 29 **Snails at Grasmere**

I was on my way home from being sacked from the college when I met Walter Sandham who lived at the bottom of the road I lived in, and told him what had happened to me. He said that staff were needed at Milligan's nursery; the pay was £5 a week there. I replied that that was much more than what I had been getting. So I walked down to the nursery, found the owner Mrs Milligan, and told her that I had been sacked for being late.

"Well, we are short of staff. You can start here on Monday." And added: "But you will have to try and keep better timing."

To begin with, there were 'red tape' problems. I could not get the usual papers from the college for keeping my tax and national insurance affairs in good order. I went to see Mr McVeigh at the unemployment office in Windermere and told him that I could not get my papers. He was very prompt in getting the matter sorted out for me.

Mrs Milligan had a wealth of knowledge about rose trees, grafting, ornamental plants, etc. And in addition to working in the nursery, she used to hire out her staff to work in the gardens of private houses.

I had not been working for very long at the nursery before we were sent to a private house called Michael's Nook in the village of Grasmere, the home of Dr and Mrs MacAlpine. Three days after we had started there, we were sitting in the garage eating our lunch when the foreman Walter Sandham said to me: "After your dinner, I want you to get a corock (which is a sort of hoe) and pull all those snails off the rocks opposite."

"What I should do with them." I asked.

"You had better put them in the dustbins, and then go to the kitchen to get hot water. Take the two metal watering cans that you will find in the greenhouse and get them full of hot water to scald the snails."

After I had had my lunch, I fetched the watering cans and was making my way to the kitchen when Mrs Macalpine met me and asked: "Boy, where do you think you are going with those watering cans?"

"I'm going to the kitchen, madam, to fill them with hot water."

"What do you want hot water for, boy?"

"Well, madam, I have to scald the snails which I have taken off the rocks opposite the garage and put them into dustbins. The foreman Mr Sandham told me to do it after I had had my lunch."

She had been carrying a basket with flowers in it and secateurs in her hand. She threw them to the ground and said: "Come and show me what you have been doing." We came to where the dustbins were. "Take those dustbins back to the rocks and empty them out, and get on your bicycle back to Ambleside."

When I got back to the nursery, Mrs Milligan said: "I know why you are back here because Mrs MacAlpine has been on the telephone and told me what has happened."

I had not been back for long before Walter Sandham and George Whitham were also back. We then learned the reason for our early return: the snails were edible (French). They were very large and being grown for food.

Bill Hargraves was another member of the staff at Milligan's nursery. The site is now a cul-de-sac of bungalows on Borrans Road.

--- ooooo ---

Features of Ambleside

This stoop or gatepost in the wall of the fish and chip shop in The Slack marks where tolls used to be charged for using The Slack as a thoroughfare.

These premises were in earlier times Charles Creighton's blacksmiths shop.

Chapter 30 **Sunshine recorders and water samples**

Few people know that sunshine recorders used to be sited on several fells around Ambleside, for example: Wansfell, Nab Scar, Low Pike, Loughrigg, and Kirkstone. They had to be attended to every day because each recording card lasted for only one day. Staff from the council offices such as Arnold Burrows and Miss Vera Bunting and a member of the Stevenson family in The Slack used to do this.

The recorders were made of brass and glass, and were about 10 inches (25 cm) high. The glass part was a ball shape. Around half of the ball was a curved brass plate which held a card in place at a constant distance from the glass. When the sun shone, its rays passed through the glass and burned a trace on the card, like a brown line. The recorders were usually fixed to rock.

A local man named Fred Prickett used to use a trailer and a dinghy to collect samples of water and other things from the lakes and take them to the Freshwater Biological Association at Ferry House to expand the knowledge and understanding of the local area. Traps were used in many of the lakes. I helped him from time to time with all sorts of samples.

I remember using a torch at night to watch with him as large numbers of elvers (young eels) crossed the road under Loughrigg. They were on their migration between local rivers and the Sargasso Sea.

Fred made many things from wood, including walking sticks. He also made a back scratcher which he used later in hospital to scratch inside his plaster.

Mr Smyly and Mr Fry were among the staff of the Freshwater Biological Association known to me.

--- ooooo ---

The bungalow at the bottom of the drive of the Hollbeck Ghyll Hotel.

Chapter 31 **At Holbeck Ghyll**

Holbeck Ghyll was a private home when I worked there, with tennis courts, a putting green, and two orchards as well as flower beds, lawns, trees, etc. I spent about 25 years there in total. This included my national service in the army.

It was not very long after I started working at Holbeck Ghyll that my mother said she could not keep me in food and clothes on thirty shillings (£1.50) a week. So I went to the housekeeper, Miss Collins, and told her that I wanted to see the boss.

"What for?" was her response.

I told her I wanted an increase in pay, and she said she would pass on my request to see the boss.

A few days went by. Beatrice, a member of the house staff, came out on to the front lawn shouting my name. Having found me, she told me the boss would see me at 6.30pm on Friday in the blue room. "And do not be late."

I arrived early at the front door and rang the bell. On finding me on the doorstep, the butler said that I did not go into the house by the front door but by the servants' entrance round the back. After making my way to the back door, I was shown into the blue room, and sat down to wait.

"Who told you to sit down?" were the first words of the boss. I stood up. I then explained the purpose of my visit. Not only did I garden for the usual hours during the week, it was necessary to tend the boilers on Saturdays and Sundays as well. And there was the regular task of bringing in coal and logs for the seven fires in the house.

He replied that he and his wife would have a serious discussion about the matter and then let me know what the decision was.

Many days went by before Beatrice came out on to the lawn, shouting my name. Her message was the same as before: 6.30pm on Friday in the blue room, and not to be late. I arrived early at the back door and was shown into the blue room once again. (I knew exactly where the blue room was because we had taken the carpet out from there to the field to beat it.). I did not sit down this time but remained standing while i waited.

"My wife and I have given your request very serious consideration." said the boss when he came in. "We are to give you an extra £1 per week. And we expect you to work hard for it. Now, be gone."

I thanked him and departed.

What a mess

One Saturday morning I was working in the greenhouse when the head gardener, Mr Pringle, had to go down to the bungalow at the bottom of the drive for something. He left me in the greenhouse tying up tomato plants and potting houseplants. Suddenly, the greenhouse door was thrown open and every pane of glass in it broke. Standing there was the boss in a fierce rage.

"Where is Pringle?" I told him he had gone down to the bungalow for something.

"Get yourself down there. I want to see him straight away."

I ran to get Mr Pringle and told him the boss was in a fierce rage about something. He asked: "Did he tell you what it was about?", and I said: "No." He put on his jacket and came up to the greenhouse where the boss was standing waiting for him.

"I told you last week that I was expecting guests this weekend and I wanted everything to be absolutely perfect."said the boss. "And what do I find when I go down to the putting green and tennis courts and the bottom garden? I find everywhere covered in sewage, so come down and see what a mess it is."

We went down the drive to the putting green and tennis courts as the Rolls Royces and Bentleys were arriving with the visitors. He said: "Look, Middleton! You get on your bike to Ambleside and go to Mr Jennings' yard and get him to bring the two-handed pump."

So I went on my bike into Ambleside to Mr Jennings' yard, which was closed. But Mr Jennings was in the office in Back Compston (Compston Street). He said: "You will have to go and get Billy Dixon to get the wagon out again and take the pump up for you." I knew where Billy Dixon lived on North Road and I managed to catch him at home, so he got the wagon out, put the pump on it, and took it up to Holbeck Ghyll. There the pump was taken down to the sewage tank.

We proceeded to pump out the water to clean the tank. When we had pumped the tank out and looked inside, it was in a condition far worse than we had expected.

The boss was talking to Mr Pringle. I think he was going to sack him, whereupon Mr Pringle produced his diary and found the date we had last emptied the septic tank which was only a few months earlier. The boss wanted to know what had upset the working of the tank, and I remembered the housekeeper Miss Collins saying that when I washed the dog yard out where the dogs were I had to use Domestos in future, or if I cleaned the yard I had to use Domestos. Mr Pringle told the boss about this. The boss immediately went to see the housekeeper and gave her the sack, because he blamed the Domestos for stopping the tank from working properly.

The first year I worked at Holbeck Ghyll I went into the tank. It was a mosaic of coloured bacteria. When I came out I was completely covered from head to foot. Mr Pringle said: "Don't worry. When you come into the light they will all drop off." And they did.

The holly tree with no berries

There was a giant holly tree just outside the potting shed which I had seen have berries only once, not year after year.

We had a new head gardener Ted Mason when Mr Pringle left. Ted said that the tree should have berries every year but the pollen was not being blown to it when the male tree was in blossom. We would have to keep an eye on the male tree so that we could cut a bough out of it for fertilising the tree which had no berries.

Once the male tree was in full blossom, a ladder was placed in it and a large bough was cut from it and lowered gently to the ground. The bough and the ladder were taken to the tree without berries. The ladder was placed in the tree. The bough was tied high up in the tree and given a vigorous shake to release some of the pollen. Further scattering of the pollen was left to the wind.

It worked. The tree without berries had a profusion of berries the next autumn. We did the same thing every year Ted Mason was there. The boss was very pleased to see the berries but we never made him any the wiser as to what we had done.

A cosy corner

It was always warm in the melon house. And it was not unknown for me to fall asleep in there at the end of the day if I sat down for a while.

--- ooooo ---

Features of Ambleside

Ambleside has several lamp posts resembling the days when they were lit by gas from the local gasworks.

This one stands at the junction of Nook Road and Smithy Brow.

Chapter 32 **Paper bags, little boxes, and a railway wagon at Kendal Station**

My employment at Holbeck Ghyll was interrupted by the severe winter of 1963/64. so I went to sign on the dole at the local office in Windermere for unemployment money.

Sitting behind the desk was Mr McVeigh. He was small in stature, and a cigarette - half of it ash - hung from the corner of his mouth.

“What do you want?” was the greeting I received.

“I've come to sign on for dole money.”

“You can't do that. There are jobs about. There's one in Kendal at Airey's. Take this card and go on the bus to find out about it. Here's some money to pay your fare.” He gave me 9d, about 4p.

I arrived at the shop on Allhallows Lane, looked inside through the window, and had a quick look round as I went in. Standing behind the counter were two men dressed in the brown coats worn by so many shopkeepers. They were indeed the owners, father and son.

“Splendid.” was their reply when I told them I had come from Ambleside to enquire about a job. “Come round to the back of the counter.”

I had thought that I would be working in the shop – a typical ironmongery business. But they took me through a door to what I assumed would be the back of the shop.

What a surprise I got. They asked me to put on a face-mask. A woman was busy pouring small amounts of powder into small paper bags. These were then carefully sealed and placed neatly into cardboard boxes.

“But this is not all we do.”

Going through another door I was asked to keep the facemask on. We went into a room where soap was being made. Colourings and scents were added to the basic ingredients to make different batches. When finished, the bars of soap were carefully packed and they too were placed in cardboard boxes.

Going through yet another door we came to where shoe polish was being made.

And in another room candles were being made, with yet more colours and sizes. I had wondered why there were so many balls of string until I realised that they were the wicks for the candles.

To a newcomer, the dustiness of the powder room and the smells were almost overpowering.

I had discovered a hive of industry behind an ordinary-looking shop.

And the railway wagon at Kendal railway station? This displayed the firm's name on its sides and periodically it was filled as full as possible with the products made in the various rooms. The wagon was then sent, for example to London, to supply local businesses with new stock. The candles, I learned, were also sent abroad.

I worked at Airey's until the end of the winter and then returned to Holbeck Ghyll.

--- ooooo ---

Features of Ambleside

The shelter in the corner of Borrans Park.

It is mentioned on page 33.

Chapter 33 **Cats up the chimney**

Heavy rain often causes flooding. Thus it was at Rothay Holme one winter near the Scout hut. My mother and I had walked down there to see what had been happening. Her attention was caught by a meowing sound coming from an apple tree.

“Look, George! There's a little kitten in that tree. Do you think you can rescue it? Please be careful.”

I waded into the water - it came above my knees – and I was able to rescue the kitten. We took it home for it to recover from its ordeal. We named it Kitty.

She had several litters of kittens which we always managed to find. And then she had a litter that we could not find however much we searched. We knew they had been born because of the change in her size.

“I don't know where Kitty's kittens are.” said mother to me. “I can't find them anywhere.”

Hunt as we might, there was no sign of them.

I was coming home from work and happened to look up at the house. And there was Kitty climbing into the top of one of the chimneys. I told mother what I had seen, and she asked me to climb up and get them out. My hands got very scratched as I picked them out one by one.

The kittens were not new-born because their eyes were open. They were given away to local farms when they were old enough.

--- ooooo ---

Features of Ambleside

This scene was probably unique: a telephone box with its own, exclusive parking space.

The location is at the bottom of The Struggle.

The telephone box has been removed and the notices on the post changed.

This was the middle notice on the post.

The top one stated that parking was limited to 30 minutes between 8am and 6pm, and no return within 1 hour.

The bottom one required the display of a parking disc, available from local businesses.

Chapter 34 **Furniture in the road**

While pushing my bike up Park Street after work one evening I came across a large collection of furniture in the road. I noticed that the door of house number 6 was open. And it was beginning to rain.

On looking inside there was a woman sitting on a chair with her head in her hands, in a virtually empty room. I asked gently if anything was wrong.

"Oh dear," she said. "I said to the man that I wanted him to be careful with the furniture and not knock it as it came in."

""Right, Charlie," he said to his mate, "We're off." and they climbed into the van and disappeared."

"Well," I said, "If you tell me where you would like the furniture putting. I will move it for you. But first I must go and get something to cover the furniture to keep the rain off."

Some of the items were very heavy but eventually everything was out of the rain and indoors as she wished.

She was very adamant that she should pay me for what I had done. And I was equally adamant that she would not. "You are a new neighbour." I said.

"Would you like a glass of my own homemade peach wine?" she asked.

"Yes, please. That sounds very nice."

So we sat down and had a glass, and then she insisted that I take a bottle home with me.

Now Uncle Harry and Aunty Doris lived next door to the lady whose name I had learned was Mrs Summers. Within a few days of her moving in, he was taken seriously ill and had to go to Kendal hospital. Aunty Doris was not happy travelling there by bus on her own. I took her in my van instead. But it broke down so I went on the bus with her.

A few more days had passed when Mrs Summers stopped me and asked where I was going. I explained what had happened, and to my surprise she said: "Why not use my car?"

“I've never driven an automatic before. And its new.” was my reply.

“Take me to Grasmere to see how you get on.” she said.

“There,” she said when we got back. “You can use my car. Just park it where it was when you have finished.”

She surprised me again after Aunty Doris and I had returned from visiting Uncle Harry. “You keep the keys and use the car as you need,” she said “If I want to use it, I will come and get the keys from you.”

And that is how things were until Uncle Harry died.

--- ooooo ---

Features of Ambleside

This sign stands at the bottom of The Struggle.

It does not say that it is nearly 3 miles (5 km) to the Kirkstone Pass at the top.
The increase in altitude is about 1,100 feet (300m)’
The bottom section of the sign lights up when the road is closed.

Chapter 35 **Snowcem at Carr Crag**

The time had come for the house to be redecorated on the outside – not a small task.

The owner was surprised to find out just how much it would cost to be done by a professional decorator.

“We'll do it ourselves, George.” was his conclusion.

It was not long before he went and bought the drums of white snowcem, and, in due course, he took the lids off the drums and laid the lids to one side in getting ready to start the job.

When I arrived later that morning I noticed that there was a trail of white marks leading to the house. I looked through a window and could see many more marks inside on the carpets and on the furniture.

Nobody had seen me and I decided that I did not want to be involved in cleaning up. It looked as though it would be a long job. So I decided to make a hasty retreat before anybody saw me.

I learned later that the two young children had found the open drums and then had fun as children do when they find things that they should not have found.

--- ooooo ---

Chapter 36 **Owls went to market**

A fluffy ball on the side of the road at night is an unusual sight. But that is what I saw one night on the main road in Windermere near Carriage Drive. I stopped my van, got out, and went back to have a closer look. Four eyes were looking back at me.

The fluffy ball was, in fact, two tiny owls almost far enough on to the road to be killed by the traffic. I picked them up and found a safe spot for them in my van until I got home.

What should I do – keep them or not?

I telephoned the RSPCA for help. Mr McNeill said that they would prefer that I take them to one of their centres. I said that I would like to keep them because I was familiar with country life and confident that I could manage. He agreed that I could. For food, he said that I should get in touch with a local hatchery and ask them to send me dead chicks. And to get the owls' digestion going properly they should also have fresh meat. So I was advised to trap mice – though the RSPCA did not welcome killing anything.

I found a wooden box and got a piece of netting from Tinny Martin's to put over the top to keep them in. They continued to thrive and grow, and developed into beautiful birds.

Mother was not pleased with the nuisance they caused.

I regularly had a stall at Barrow-in-Furness market for my plants, shrubs, trees etc. The owls were very tame and I had the idea of taking them with me to sit at the back of the stall – they might attract customers. Mother said she would not come with me in the van because of the smell they made.

They sat on the back of the stall under a cover to keep them relatively in the dark, spending most of their time apparently asleep. I became popular with the children who asked their parents if they could look at the owls. Many of the children did indeed go round the back of the stall to look at them.

At night at home, I used to sit them one on each of my shoulders and take them down to the Kelsick field to let them fly on long pieces of string. Sometimes they caught a mouse or vole easily, and sometimes it took an hour or two. On moonless nights they usually caught nothing. Eventually, they flew without the strings.

After five years, one of them died. I did not know the cause but had noticed that its droppings had become different from the normal colour and smell.

The other one thrived. One night, after 10 years or so, I took it down to the field as usual. A distant hoot came from Loughrigg. The one on my shoulder was almost in a frenzy as it looked this way and that and up and down. It hooted in reply, obviously right close to my ear. There was another hoot in the distance and my owl replied again. And then it flew off, silent in its flight as always. I walked round the field for the rest of the night but it did not return. I went back to the field the next night. There was hooting in the distance but no owl came near me.

I never recognised the owl again although owls have sat in the tree at home many times. Over the years since the disappearance of my owl, those in the tree may well have been younger generations of the two which gave me so much enjoyment.

--- ooooo ---

Chapter 37 **Holly was needed**

From one year to the next, as soon as Christmas was over I started to put moss on to frames for wreaths. I made many hundreds which were taken to market. I used to go round my cousins' farms to collect the material for them. The moss came from the fells; and the greenery and holly were collected nearer Christmas.

When I came to look for berried holly in 1977, I was devastated to find that, after going round all the places where I normally went, there was hardly any to be found anywhere. It got to two or three weeks before Christmas and I did not know what I was going to do.

One night my parents said to me: "Are you not going dancing anywhere tonight?" And I said that I might go and see my cousins in Windermere. So I did. I said to Geoff: "I don't know what I'm going to do. I have hundreds of wreaths to make and I have very little berried holly to do them with."

"Well, George." said Geoff, "I know where there is a tree not far from here which is absolutely loaded with red berries. But the lady who owns it will not let you have one berry off it. She can be very difficult to deal with."

I said to Geoff: "I am so desperate for some berried holly. You must take me to see the lady."

Then Ursula, Geoff's wife said: "You must take him because he is not going to give up about it."

Geoff put on his hat and coat and said: "I will take you to the drive but that is as far as I will take you. You do not know the lady like I do. I have known her since I was a young boy."

He took me to the drive entrance: "That's it. You go yourself to see her. I am going no further."

I set off up the drive and noticed the lovely holly tree and also some pernettia bushes with red, pink and white berries. As I made my way round a bend in the drive I was met by water running down the side. The mansion was now in view and I could see that the water was seeping through the walls and coming out under the front door. I went to the door and knocked on the door knocker. Nobody came to the door so I tried to open it. It opened to reveal plaster and water all over the mosaic floor. Part of the ceiling had fallen down, and a lot of water was running down the fine staircase. I knocked on various doors and got no answer from any of them. Each opened to a scene of water falling on beautiful furniture and fabrics.

I went along a passage and opened a door to find the kitchen. Sitting there with her head in her hands and crying was, I presumed, the lady of the house. I approached her and said: "Can I help you turn the water off? Where are the stop taps?"

"There are some under the sink but I don't know where all of them are" she said.

I turned off the taps under the sink, and then went and turned of the electricity supply. I then went to look for stop tap keys in case I needed them for other stop taps because the water was still running. I found some in a small room and took them out into a small yard where I saw covers for some taps. I closed the taps and went back indoors to check the result. The water was still running.

I went back into the little room to hunt again and found a very large stop tap key. I took it out into what is known locally as Shammy's Lane. There I found a stop tap which the key fitted and I turned it as much as I could. I went back indoors to see if there was any improvement. Yes. The water had stopped running.

A neighbour had followed me in and asked what I was doing there.

"Don't upset the plumber." said the lady of the house. "He has just turned the water off and done a wonderful job."

I said: "I am not the plumber."

The lady of the house said: "What are you doing here?"

"Well," I said, "my cousin Geoff told me you had a lovely berried holly tree. And I saw some lovely pernettia bushes in your garden. I am here to ask you if I could have some of the berried holly, please, to put on the wreaths that I make."

"You can have all the berries off the holly and the other bushes too. I can't thank you enough."

The neighbour had disappeared during the conversation but then returned to tell us that I had turned off the supply to the nearby houses as well as the mansion.

Then the plumber arrived, and said: "Oh, you have turned the water off."

I said: "Yes, now it is up to you. I only came to see if I could have some berried holly for my wreaths. The lady of the house has said I can have as much as I need from the tree and the bushes for turning off the water."

I was very grateful indeed.

--- ooooo ---

Features of Ambleside

Ambleside has modern buffers as well as the ancient ones.

These ones were installed recently in Old Lake Road.

Chapter 38 **Dilapidated greenhouses at Calgarth**

When I was no longer able to use the gardens at Crow How (which is on the road from Ambleside to Rydal), I was temporarily at a loss as to where I would take everything that was capable of being moved. Then I learned that Major Hedley had some unused greenhouses at Calgarth. So I went to see him. I was wearing my gardening clothes and wellington boots.

The front door was opened by the butler, Mr Taylor, who asked what I wanted. I introduced myself and said that I wanted to see Major Hedley, and was asked what about. I said that I wanted to talk about using the greenhouses, to which Mr Taylor replied that he did not think Major Hedley would see me. At that moment, Major Hedley was coming down the stairs and called out: "Taylor, who is at the door?"

"A Mr Middleton wants to talk about using the greenhouses, sir."

"Show him in to the green room, please."

I mentioned that I was not really dressed for that but he said that he too came into the house wearing gardening clothes and dirty boots.

After I had explained my circumstances, he pulled the bell chord and asked the member of staff who came into the room to bring coffee and biscuits for us.

He told me that the greenhouses were in a very poor state with most of the glass missing. They needed new glass, puttying and repainting. But the boiler was in good order and there was plenty of coke to fire it and heat the greenhouses when they were ready for use again. Taylor responded to another pull of the bell chord and he was asked to bring the Austin Healey Sprite to the front door. "Tell Townsend that he won't be needed because I will drive Mr Middleton to the greenhouses myself."

It was then that he asked me what my Christian name was. "George, sir."

"Good. That makes it more friendly. I will take George to the greenhouses myself."

They were indeed quite dilapidated and it was obvious that a lot of work would be required before they were fully usable again. I told him that I thought that my father would help me although he was over 70 years old. The major asked me if I was still serious about taking on such a task. I replied that I was. He then surprised me by saying that he would provide all the glass, putty and paint that would be necessary.

When we were back in the house I said that he had not mentioned what rent he expected for the use of the greenhouses. He said that paying rent was a business-like attitude and £200 a year would not be unreasonable. But he was an extremely wealthy man and had no need of more money. He would let me use the greenhouses for the next two years without paying any rent; I would be putting in a lot of work in making them usable again. After further thought, he said he would increase the time to three years.

Eventually, I used the greenhouses for about 14 years until the 1980s.

--- ooooo ---

Anne and myself at an Ambleside event a few years ago. GM

Anne seems to be listening to my rosette.

Chapter 39 **Social event at Bowness-on-Windermere**

A social event that I particularly remember was a New Year's dance at Bowness-on-Windermere more than 50 years after the event at Hawkshead recorded in chapter 23 involving Mrs Heelis (Beatrix Potter).

I was with my partner Anne and we had had a very enjoyable evening. I decided to book a taxi to take us back to Ambleside. It was very cold when I got outside and slippery under foot because of frost. A local policeman was standing nearby and he promptly told me, on learning that I wanted to book a taxi to take us home, that there were no taxis. He said there was so much black ice on the roads that there was no traffic at all.

I went back inside with a worried look on my face, wondering how we would get back to Ambleside in conditions bad enough to stop all traffic; walking home would not be sensible. I told Anne what I had found out.

Other people must also have heard about how bad the conditions outside were. A man from further down the room came over and asked: "What is the trouble, George?"

I told him and he instantly said: "Don't worry. Your mother gave us a home when I was a baby. Stay with us tonight and I will see that you get home tomorrow."

It was Michael Pointer.

We got home safely the next day without any trouble.

--- ooooo ---

Chapter 40 **Window cleaning? Rocking horses?**

I was enjoying a midday meal in the Central Cafe (now Daisy's Cafe) one day when a young woman came in and ordered a drink.

Seeking to strike up a conversation with her, I said that it was unusual to order just a drink at that time of day. She was very honest and replied that she did not have enough money to pay for food. She was out of work and sleeping rough because she could not pay her share of the flat she had been living in. I said that I would pay for something for her to eat, and it was not long before she too was enjoying herself.

Our conversation continued and we started to talk about the future. One of my suggestions was that she could try window cleaning. This surprised her: "Don't talk rubbish. That isn't suitable for a woman."

We met again the following day in the cafe, but not by arrangement. She had been thinking about cleaning windows and still had doubts about such a job. What did she need to do it; where should she start. I said she could borrow my ladders and a bucket to start with, and a chamois leather could be got from Tinny Martin's hardware shop in Compston Road. As for where should she start, there were several houses in Millans Park where I felt sure the people would welcome having their windows cleaned.

So began a new business. She quickly made enough money to settle her debt and to buy some ladders inexpensively at a farm sale.

I met her again after a considerable time and asked how the business was progressing. She told me that they had ceased cleaning house windows and did supermarkets only.

Making rocking horses started in a very similar way, with me enjoying a meal in the Central Cafe. A young man I had met at market came into the cafe and we got into conversation. He was an unemployed joiner and had decided to spend the day in and around Ambleside. He was looking for work. I knew about what he had done in the past and, after a few moments of thought, suggested that he became self employed. What could he make? I suggested that rocking horses might be something worthwhile.

A few months later we met again. He said he had made one and asked if I would have a look at it. I did so and had to tell him that it was not good enough. He could make it look much better if, for example, the saddle was of leather and the tail of horse hair; in other words, more realistic. He was not pleased with me.

Several weeks passed. He then told me that he hoped he had made enough changes for me to be satisfied. I went and looked at the new horse. He had.

I do not remember whether he made 10 or 12 but it was something like that. Christmas was approaching and he took them to market. He sold every one.

The Central Buildings.

Daisy's Cafe is between the shops painted red and green.

--- ooooo ---

Chapter 41 **Space for my plants, trees, etc**

John Parsons allowed me to put a hen house in Cicely Woods because I helped him at hay time until I went to work for a Mr Fielding. He allowed me to use his field which was up Sweden Lane.

I then moved to Calgarth Gardens. When I had to move from there I went to see Mr Wade. I asked him if there was any land I could use as a garden and to keep hens. He was chairman of the council and he said he would put my need to the council. I received a letter from him telling me that there were allotments on the council land at Rothay Holme. I moved my things there.

While coming home from market one day I noticed a group of men who were walking about among my plants and trees and other things. I went over to them and asked them what they were doing. I was ignored.

“It's nothing to do with you. This piece of ground is going to be sold to Mr Standing for a warehouse.”

I said to them that I had several years lease on the land.

“What lease? You have to be off this land. There are no receipts for rent or a lease.”

So I went hot foot to the solicitor and knocked on the door. The secretary said the solicitor was busy but I said it was urgent that I saw him.

“What is the problem?” he asked.

“There are some men on the piece of land I use saying I have to be off it in two weeks and that there are no receipts for rent or a lease.”

The solicitor rang a bell. The clerk came in. “Please get Mr Middleton's file for me.”

He looked at the papers briefly and said “That's what they think, is it? Get in the Jaguar.”

They were still walking round when we arrived.

“Tell Mr Middleton to get off in a fortnight?” he said to them. “Where will he go? Mr Middleton has you 'over a barrel'. He has receipts and a lease for seven years. There are still four years to go.”

The solicitor was asked to hand over the papers there and then.

He refused but agreed to send copies to the council.

A few days later a letter arrived from the council. It conceded that the council was, indeed, in a very difficult position because the land had already been sold for warehouse development. The council had other pieces of land which I could look at once they had sent me the details. One was in Kendal where the canal had been filled in; it was most unsuitable. Another piece was a field at Grasmere with the remains of large oak trees; it too was not suitable. Other pieces were at Staveley (between Windermere and Kendal), Windermere and Bowness-on-Windermere. The only place in Ambleside was the field on Castle Field. I went to look at it with a councillor and decided to take it.

However, I wanted to keep the piece of land where I had the garden previously. They were very reluctant but I persisted that I wanted it. When I told the solicitor he said that he would see what he could do, but he thought that I had a fairly good deal with the big plot. I might not get much more out of the deal.

For me, moving a well established garden would be difficult.

The council sent me plans of two pieces of land, one with plants and the other on Castle Field.

The Scout people approached my solicitor with a request to build a Scout hut. He sent me a letter saying that they could build a hut only if I agreed. I did so. I lent a hand when the building started and told the architect that the area was subject to flooding. I did not think that the footings for the hut were high enough. They were raised a little but the increased height proved ineffective in preventing the hut from being flooded.

--- ooooo ---

Chapter 42 **Taken to court and fined three times**

The area outside my home at the end of Park Street has always been known in the family as 'the yard'. My family has used it since my mother and father moved there before Uncle Billy was born. Until 2010 it was unmade but was tarmaced and six parking bays were painted on it and clearly marked with the identity of the homes they belong to. In making these changes my beech hedge was removed and a six-foot fence erected in its place.

I started parking my car or van in the yard when I bought my first vehicle, a Ford Thames van from Scott's garage in 1961. I also used part of the yard for my plants, shrubs, pots, etc used in my gardening work

After many years of such use, some of my neighbours objected to it.

In 2005 they took me to court. The first thing I knew about it was when a bailiff pushed summons papers in my face while I was eating a meal in the restaurant at Morrison's supermarket in Kendal.

In court, the judge said he was fining me for trespassing with my van, and giving permission for the removal of all my possessions there. I said that I had used the yard since starting with gardening.

"Button it," said the judge "Or I will send you down for two years for contempt of my court."

The result was that I was fined £1,500. Costs were awarded against me. Everything of mine in the yard, including my van, was removed. Police saw that I did not touch anything.

About two years later, an objection was raised about our dustbin being in the yard. I told the judge that our dustbin had been in the yard since the days of my parents. The result of the case was the same: a fine of £1,500 with costs being awarded against me.

About two weeks later, a summons was served on me for using a clothes line in the yard. On this occasion it was served on me while I was having a drink in the Chocolate Bar in Millans Park, Ambleside. The result of the case was as before: a fine of £1,500 with costs being awarded against me.

I had not been able to afford legal representation at any of the court hearings, and had no funds for paying the costs. The court decided that the two pieces of land which I owned should be sold, and the money raised would pay the costs.

In due course I received a cheque for £50, the balance after paying the costs but not the three fines of £1,500 each. I did not cash the cheque.

--- ooooo ---

Features of Ambleside

Waterhead, where Ambleside meets Windermere.

Wraysholme, where the Maypole was erected in the garden.

Three scenes from the Rushbearing Procession on 6 July 2012 -

including Mrs Jessie Wilson at the age of 101 carrying her flower-bedecked rushes, and her nephew Vernon Rigg.

Chapter 43 **Festivals**

May Day at Wraysholme

It is many years since there was a May Day festival in Ambleside.

I recall that Mrs O'Brien from Millans Park used to organise the event. The Maypole was erected on the lawn and became the focus of the dancing. There was also a procession around the town for the May Queen.

Three of the girls who were May Queen were Elsie and Joan Barton and Diana Tyson. Their attendants included Peter Fletcher.

Vera Bunting used to go round Ambleside with a dressed doll for a 'Guess the name of the doll' competition and with raffle tickets. The funds raised went towards the Merrylegs Foundation which supported the festival.

Rushbearing

The carrying of decorated bearings as in the pictures opposite in procession around Ambleside has not ceased. It takes place on the first Saturday of July each year.

The procession and short service which follows it commemorate the time when church floors were plain earth and covered with rushes. These were cleaned out once a year and then replaced by new ones.

There is a large mural in St Mary's Church of a rushbearing procession which was painted towards the end of the Second World War as a token of thanks to the people of Ambleside for being 'home' to the Royal College of Art during the war.

--- ooooo ---

Ambleside Parish Centre.

A snowflake, one of the decorative panels on the centre's towers.

Inside St Mary's Church.

Chapter 44 **Ambleside in the 21st century**

The Lake District in the north west of England is among the most beautiful places in the world. Those of us who live here enjoy the magnificent surroundings all the time. Many millions of people come here each year to share and benefit from the wonder that nature presents to us.

Ambleside, nestling at the northern end of Windermere, has a long history. I have not researched its history and much of it has not been recorded. But I hope that this small book will be an encouragement to many people to come and find out what the town and the surrounding area have to offer in so many ways in the 21st century, and to look into its past as well.

Ambleside continues to thrive. It has a wide range of businesses for a relatively small community, including but not restricted to: two butchers, three small supermarkets (the third one opened in December 2011), fruit and vegetable shops, art shops, branches of two banks and a building society, a county council library, the Armitt Museum and Library, two chemists, three cinemas (one owner), many shops selling clothing etc for outdoor activities, a large garden centre, three bookshops, a post office and tourist information centre, a hardware/ironmonger store, a wide range of restaurants and cafes to suit many different tastes, an indoor climbing wall, newsagents, and many hotels, bed and breakfast businesses and holiday homes.

Another aspect of Ambleside's life is the local college. This is now part of the University of Cumbria, having been part of the University of Lancaster. For a long time it was the independent St Martin's College after having been known by the much earlier local name of Charlotte Mason College. Many business and outdoor courses are available at the Ambleside campus.

The parish centre, Ambleside Parish Centre to give it its proper name, was opened in 2006 after a lengthy period of fundraising. It has a unique position next to the parish church and overlooking Rothay Park. The decorative stonework was carved by the local craftsman Danny Clahane and reflects the location and purpose of the building: fish, birds, trees, wind, fire, water, and a snowflake are all among the things depicted on the different panels. The building was designed by the local architect Paul Grout. The main contractor was the local firm Cox and Allen. And the building is for the use of the local community and beyond.

A large proportion of the funds for the new centre came from the sale of the Methodist Church and Hall. The congregation of the Methodist Church had been considering renewing the interior of the church, and found that it would cost much more than could be raised even if the church hall was sold. The minister at the time was Rev Richard Hall. He suggested that the Methodist congregation could worship in the new centre to be built next to the parish church. The suggestion met with general approval. The plans for the centre were duly modified to accommodate the congregation.

The National Lottery also made a very substantial contribution to the cost of the building.

The Methodist church building and hall were subsequently redeveloped and became much-needed homes for local people, and are now known as Wesley Court.

St Mary's Church has undergone a major transformation inside. It was re-opened in September 2010. The pews and the floor of the nave were removed. A new floor was laid and the building was cleaned from top to bottom, including the stained glass windows. An office, a small kitchen, and toilets were included in the new design. The drawings for the work were prepared by George Walker, a member of the congregation. He played a significant role during the work, and died some six months after the building was re-opened.

Businesses in Ambleside continue to change from time to time. When this particular chapter was being prepared there were very few empty business premises in the town. The Homes of Football has moved to the Urbis building in Manchester with the National Football Museum, and the branch of the HSBC Bank closed recently.

--- ooooo ---

Names of people and businesses

Place names